THE EPISTLE TO THE HEBREWS

THE EPISTLE
TO THE HEBREWS

AN HISTORICAL AND THEOLOGICAL RECONSIDERATION

THE BAIRD LECTURE, 1949

BY

WILLIAM MANSON

B.A. (Oxon), D.D. (Knox College, Toronto), D.D. (Glasgow)
Professor of Biblical Criticism in the
University of Edinburgh

HODDER AND STOUGHTON LTD.
WARWICK SQUARE, LONDON, E.C.4

First published . *June* 1951
Third impression . . 1957

Made and Printed in Great Britain for HODDER AND STOUGHTON LTD.
by T. AND A. CONSTABLE LTD., Printers, Edinburgh

PREFACE

THE present volume incorporates a series of lectures undertaken at the invitation of the Baird Lectureship Trustees, and delivered in the Martin Hall, New College, Edinburgh, in February 1950. I desire cordially to thank the Trustees for the honour conferred on me by the invitation and for their consent to my request under stress of other duties to defer the delivery of the lectures from the autumn of 1949 to the following spring. I wish also to acknowledge the kindness of the Principal and Senate of New College in making the Martin Hall available at the time.

The reasons which have led me to undertake a reconsideration of the purpose of the Epistle are stated in some detail in the opening chapter of the book. As a New Testament teacher I have for long been dissatisfied with the direction which critical thought, principally associated for us in this country and the English-speaking world with the names of two distinguished scholars, Professor James Moffatt and Professor E. F. Scott, has taken with regard to Hebrews during the last half-century. Whereas the older criticism understood the Epistle to reflect a phase or crisis in the evolution of Jewish Christianity in the apostolic period, the modern theory has unhitched the Epistle from these moorings and floated it out into the mid-stream of the general life of the first-century Church, so taking it out of a supposed backwater to give it a place in the main current of Christian history. On this

13+15

interpretation the religious situation of the community addressed in Hebrews had nothing specifically to do with any attraction exercised by Judaism but was determined by some form of secular drift to irreligion or to paganism.

I cannot conceal the conviction that this right-about-face in critical opinion has involved a turning of the back on some of the most salient features of the Epistle, and has therefore brought about a clouding of the issues. The new theory starts not from the central substance of Hebrews but, as it seems to me, from peripheral features and from a number of *a priori* and not sufficiently examined assumptions regarding both Judaism and Christianity in the apostolic age. I cannot therefore think that it makes real contact with history. Indeed neither the older nor the more recent approach to the problem of Hebrews has sufficiently integrated the Epistle into the historical development of the world-mission of Christianity or brought the situation behind the letter into clear and adequate focus.

In this opinion I have become confirmed by considerations based on a fresh study of the Stephen-records in the book of the Acts of the Apostles. I am convinced that a straight line runs from the teaching and apologia of the proto-martyr to the Epistle to the Hebrews, and I believe it is to be regarded as a central line in the development of the Christian world-mission. In the present book, therefore, I have sought an approach to Hebrews which will (1) integrate the Epistle afresh into the history of the world-mission from its inception in Stephen, (2) re-evaluate the potentialities of the religious situation in such a centre of world-mission Christianity as Rome, (3) trace the connection between the doctrine of Hebrews and the theology of the world-mission as a whole, and (4) from careful study of the argument of the Epistle establish conclusions as to the situation and character of the community addressed and so recover for the Epistle its organic position in relation to first-century evangelism and life.

It is not necessary here to set out in detail the positions to which I have been led. They are indicated in outline in the closing section of Chapter I, in the summaries which conclude Chapters III and V, and in Chapter VI. The historical ground of the approach is set out in Chapter II, which deals with Stephen and his eschatology; here is indeed the pivot on which my whole argument turns. I have come to see that distinctions of a very important order have to be made within the field of the Early Christian eschatology, and that the stand taken by Stephen has been determinative of Christian theology to its furthest bounds. I have not, however, in the exposition of the relevant material of Hebrews which is undertaken in Chapters III-V attempted anything like a full commentary on the Epistle, but have confined myself to the points which bear on the above critical issues. There is, therefore, no wealth of side-reference to learned works on the more general aspects of the teaching. For myself the results of the particular inquiry on which I have concentrated attention have been to broaden the outlook both on the history—Hebrews is no mere academic treatise—and on the theology of the world-mission of Christianity in the New Testament age. If my construction of the facts is disallowed, I shall look to see it refuted; if it is defective, I trust it will be improved; if it should be thought right, I hope that even within its limits it may help at certain important points to put

Christian doctrine more squarely on the foundation of Christian history, and to show it, as I say at the end of the book, rising phoenix-like from the embers not only of Jewish legalism but of the Jewish means of grace.

W. MANSON.

University of Edinburgh,
  1st September 1950.

NOTE ON TRANSLATIONS

The rendering of the Epistle is from the author's own translation, and the same holds of passages cited from the Septuagint and other ancient texts, including verse renderings from Greek poets.

CONTENTS

CHAPTER III

CHAPTER IV

CHAPTER I

THE PROBLEM OF THE EPISTLE AND MODERN CRITICAL THOUGHT

BY its splendid eloquence, impassioned argument, and sustained elevation of religious thought the Epistle to the Hebrews has left a permanent mark on the literature and theology of the Christian Church. In respect, however, of its origin, its historical setting, and its purpose the great Epistle has remained an enigma presenting unsolved problems to our minds. Within a generation of its composition substantial fragments of its majestic language are found embedded in the letter which Clement of Rome wrote to the Corinthian Church; but of the title, authorship, and character of the source from which these borrowings were derived there is no hint in Clement. In course of time Hebrews was destined to exercise a notable influence on the language of Christian liturgy and devotion, Catholic and Reformed—nor could it be otherwise with a book so profoundly engaged with the holiness of God and with the conception of Christian life as worship; but this was an influence which could proceed without any other understanding of the Epistle than was supplied by the tradition which soon became current that Hebrews was a letter written by St. Paul to the Jews.

In fact, of this document so charged with the inspiration of the first age of Christianity, and so potent in imaginative appeal to the mind of later times, next to

A

no traces have survived in the literature of the century which immediately succeeded Clement. We must assume a period of obscurity during which any authentic tradition which existed as to the origin of the Epistle had time to disappear.

There were particular reasons for this fading out of historical tradition in the case of the Epistle to the Hebrews. The Epistle was anonymous. It was not apparently connected at first with the name or authority of any Apostle. It was not apparently known by any distinctive title. In the West, after the momentary gleams of it which appear in Clement's letter, it was drawn into the vortex of ecclesiastical controversy over discipline, and so perhaps swept to the side. The community to which it was first addressed disappeared possibly at an early date, or merged itself in the larger unity of the Church. In the East, though where and how is not known, the Epistle was adopted into the family of the Pauline letters at some date well before the close of the second century, and as Pauline, and bearing the superscription TO THE HEBREWS, it came to Alexandria. From there, through the powerful advocacy of the local tradition, the authority of Hebrews as a work of St. Paul established itself in the third century over all the Eastern Churches, and eventually, though by slow degrees, the book secured a place in the New Testament canon of the West.

Even at Alexandria, however, the origin, authorship, particular destination, and purpose of the Epistle were matters of dispute, and the questions which were then debated, though now more accurately defined and focussed, have still to engage the minds of New Testament theologians.

LITERARY, HISTORICAL, AND THEOLOGICAL
ASPECTS OF THE PROBLEM

In scope and character the problems raised by Hebrews group themselves around the three primary aspects under which, like other New Testament writings, the letter presents itself to our minds.

The Epistle is, in the first place, a literary creation, an individual structure of thought and expression, a unity and harmony of conception and design, which once took shape in a writer's mind, and by its style, matter, and moral and emotional quality bears witness to the distinctiveness of his spirit. Secondly, it is a work of historical significance in the sense that it sprang from, and reflects or registers, a contemporary situation in some quarter of the Early Christian Church and, as such, remains a memorial of an age or phase of an age. Thirdly, it is a confessional and theological document, an impressive witness to the religion of the New Testament Church. Here it rises like a massive column, a soaring grandeur of faith in the edifice of first-century Christianity, and, as such, it engages our attention and compels our wonder, whether or not we can clear away the obscurity which envelops its base and conceals the exact circumstance of its origin from our sight.

I. As regards the first or literary aspect of Hebrews, the cultured quality and distinction of its language and style have at all times commanded recognition. Origen in his day commented on the pronouncedly Hellenic character of its phraseology and composition, contrasting its merit in this respect with the less ornate diction of the Apostle Paul to whom at Alexandria the Epistle was ordinarily attributed. His words are:

'Everyone skilled to discern differences in phrase-ology will admit that the diction of the Epistle bearing the title "To the Hebrews" has nothing in it of the stamp of ordinary speech characterising the Apostle, who admitted himself to be "a man of common talk". The style of the Epistle has a more Hellenic quality. . . . If I were to give my own opinion, I should say that the conceptions are the Apostle's, but the lan-guage and style those of one who drew upon memory for the Apostle's matter and, so to speak, composed a *scholion* on his words.' [1]

Origen, in feeling the necessity of maintaining *some* connection between Hebrews and St. Paul, was heavily influenced by the strength of the tradition current at Alexandria. In our own time Dr. Adolf Deissmann wrote of Hebrews:

'It is, on account of its polished form and scholarly contents, the first example of what we can consider Christian art-literature. That means that, with this book, Christianity took the first step out of the class in which it had its roots.' [2]

According to Dr. Deissmann, Christianity had its begin-ning in the lower and middle strata of society. It was the ordinary simple people of Galilee who surrounded Jesus, and the Churches founded by St. Paul consisted of slaves, day-labourers, hand-workers, and poor folks. 'With the little book to the Hebrews', Deissmann con-tinues, 'Early Christianity stepped out of this class. . . .

[1] Eusebius, *History*, VI. 25.
[2] *The New Testament in the Light of Modern Research* (1929), pp. 51 f.

Christianity began to take up ancient philosophy and education.'

But while Hebrews by its cultivated and philosophical language and cast of thought takes good rank as literature, it is not certain that its appearance signified so abrupt a step above and beyond the ordinary level of Christian intercourse as Deissmann and Dr. J. H. Moulton, who here agrees with him, would have us believe. Across the Early Christian stage cultured teachers had always been passing—men like Barnabas, Silvanus, Apollos, Luke, Paul, and later John of Ephesus. Also there were cultivated groups of Jewish Christians and Greek Christians among the rank and file of the Church from the first days, and even among slaves and hand-workers in that age a degree of education might exist from the standpoint of which the profound Wisdom-Christology and Atonement-doctrine of Colossians or Hebrews or Romans need not have appeared altogether abstruse or unintelligible. St. Paul, at any rate, did not think so. The real question which must here concern us, however, is whether Hebrews is just a literary exercise or expatiation, just a development of speculative and esoteric ideas on the part of an individual theologian, or is grounded essentially on truths which were a part of the common Christian confession, and which, at the time when it was written, stood in vital relation to a particular situation in the history of quite ordinary people.

II. Under the other two aspects the problem raised by the Epistle admits of being more exactly and concretely stated. What was the historical situation which evoked the Epistle, and what, if any, reality attaches to its traditional title TO THE HEBREWS? Does the letter relate, as tradition has generally assumed, to a phase in the development of *Jewish* Christianity within the Church, and if so, what? Or had the situation nothing specifically to do with Jewish Christianity, and to whom, then, was the Epistle written? This problem is prescribed for us anew by a marked change in the trend of modern critical opinion with regard to Hebrews, and we shall see that numerous questions of a quite fundamental kind have to be faced before the point at issue can be settled. For example—

(*a*) Reason may be found for thinking that on neither side of the modern debate has sufficient attention been paid to, or adequate allowance made for the *complexity* of Early Christian history, or for the diversities of thought and sympathy which might co-exist in an average congregation in the first-century Church.

(*b*) A more thorough investigation than has hitherto been undertaken may be found necessary into the special character of the Church at Rome, within which there are generally admitted reasons for locating the group of persons to which the Epistle to the Hebrews was addressed.

(*c*) Incidentally it may be found important to consider whether the teaching of the Pauline Epistles—apart possibly from the Epistle to the Romans—has not been given a disproportionate emphasis, with reference to the general life of the first-century Church, by some exponents of the modern interpretation of Hebrews.

III. Very similar is the issue which confronts us when we turn to the third aspect of the Epistle, its theological teaching. The great question here concerns the central doctrine of the Epistle, its emphasis on the fulfilment and supersession by Jesus of the Jewish cultus and the sacrifices. Have we here a *gnosis*, a speculative development of thought designed merely to prove the grandeur, the finality, the absoluteness of Christianity compared with other religions? Does the interest of the Epistle lie in the realm of *ideas*, in an idealistic and intellectual presentation of Christianity, and is this the meaning of the famous words (vi. 1):

'Let us bear forwards to perfection'?

Or is it nearer the truth to say that for both the writer and the readers of Hebrews the doctrine of the Priesthood and Oblation of Christ was of the givenness and very essence of the received Christian faith; and, when he bids the readers leave behind them the first beginnings of Christian instruction and bear forwards to perfection, he is announcing not a new advance in the matter of Christian doctrine but a summons to the group to resume once more the eschatological journey of life on which they had entered at their first conversion, but from which now, for one reason or another, they were hanging back? In the latter case we shall be driven back again on a question already mentioned.

We shall have to ask whether the doctrine of St. Paul gives us the full measure of the apostolic message preached to the world in the first generation, since St. Paul does not speak of the Priesthood of Christ; and we shall have to envisage the possibility that Romans and Hebrews must be taken *together* if we are to obtain a balanced and adequate conception of the wholeness of the world-mission gospel. The bracketing of these two documents, in order to obtain a stereoscopic view of the theology of the World Church in the apostolic age, may prove the more instructive because the two

Epistles converge in the point of their being both directed to the Christian community at Rome. We shall consider this point later. Meantime it is plain that many intricate questions of historical and theological interest confront us even at the first approach to the Epistle.

PURPOSE OF THE PRESENT WORK

If, therefore, I venture to take my rush-light afresh into some of the dark corners of this obscurity, it is with the consciousness that any illumination which I may hope to offer on this or that point may only cast into deeper shadow some untouched recesses of the problem. I hope it may not be so in the event, but the risk must be taken in an experiment of this kind, and I shall have to guard my taper-flame carefully against the wind, the more so as I am constrained to go in the teeth of certain opinions widely favoured at present and confidently offered as the introduction of a new and better hope for the understanding of Hebrews. Reference has already been made to this modern re-orientation of criticism with regard to the Epistle. There has been an abandonment of the traditional view which related the letter to a crisis in the history of a group of Jewish Christians tempted in some way to relapse to Judaism. We are asked, instead, to see in the situation behind the Epistle a quite general phase in the life of the Hellenistic Church at large. As I am unable to convince myself that the latter theory either comports with the special character of the argument of Hebrews or reveals a sufficient sense of the complexities of the religious situation in the period to which the Epistle belongs, it seems to me a task of the first urgency to re-open the whole question with a view to obtaining an exacter orientation to the Epistle and its historical background.

It appears to me for one thing, and this is an essential point in my contention, that neither the older nor the modern interpretation of Hebrews has done adequate justice to the *eschatology* of the Epistle. By this I mean its supreme concentration of interest on the critical finality of the moment of time in which Christians are placed by the Gospel. For the writer to the Hebrews this moment is one which permits no dallying and no turning of the eyes backwards. He sees all things in the light of the crisis brought about by the announcement of the Eternal World in Jesus and the swift approach of the end of the present order, including the Last Judgment. He believes with the Johannine writer that 'It is the last hour',[1] with St. Paul that 'The time is foreshortened . . . the fashion of this world is passing away'.[2] Eschatology in this sense is a determination of mind or attitude according to which all life and all history are judged purely as they relate to that Ultimate Event towards which all things are now fast hastening. It is in this sense that the terms 'eschatological calling', 'eschatological tension', 'eschatological Now' will be employed in the following pages, and it will, I think, be found that a fuller appreciation of this most important aspect of the writer's thought will help towards the solution of not a few of the problems presented to us by the Epistle.

Before, however, entering on these questions, it is necessary to look a little more closely at the two sides of the modern debate, and first at the older view, in order to establish some general positions.

[1] 1 John ii. 18.   [2] 1 Corinthians vii. 29-31.

TRADITIONAL AND OLDER APPROACHES TO THE SUBJECT

It has been noticed that with the coming of the Epistle to Alexandria as part of a corpus of Pauline Letters there came also the designation of the Epistle as TO THE HEBREWS: also that the powerful support given to this tradition at Alexandria, despite reserves on the part of the theologians of the Church, notably Origen, led to the Pauline authorship of Hebrews being everywhere acknowledged in the Eastern Churches and eventually conceded also in the West. In the latter region, though the Epistle was known to Clement of Rome and shows traces of itself in Hermas and Justin Martyr—all of them teachers connected with Rome— it had not been ascribed to Paul or any Apostle, nor was it known by the title 'To the Hebrews' earlier than A.D. 200. In the extant text of what is known as the Muratorian Canon of Christian writings Hebrews is not mentioned unless it is the letter *ad Alexandrinos* to which that document alludes. The first substantial reference to the Epistle in the West after Clement is in Tertullian, who cites Hebrews as a work of Barnabas:

'Extat enim et Barnabae titulus ad Hebraeos.'[1]

Tertullian's interest in the writing lay in its strict enforcement of Church discipline, its rigorous exclusion of the possibility of any second repentance for apostates (Hebrews vi. 1 f.). He describes the author as

'Monens itaque discipulos, omissis omnibus initiis, ad perfectionem magis tendere.'

But Tertullian's ascription of the book to Barnabas— an ascription based obviously on the authority of the

[1] Tertullian, *De Pudicitia*, 20.

manuscript which he used—and his commendation of
the writer as a man of excellent authority did not give
rise to a Barnabas tradition in the Western Church.
Even when the force of Eastern influence prevailed—
von Soden cites St. Augustine's admission:

'Movet auctoritas ecclesiarum orientalium'—

there were still in the days of St. Jerome and St. Augustine some who declined to recognise Hebrews as Paul's.
The ordinary understanding, however, once the Pauline
authorship was conceded, was that the Apostle wrote
the Epistle as an appeal to the Jewish people or nation,
and this has remained the official teaching both of the
Roman and the Reformed Churches.

With the rise of modern scholarship these opinions
came under serious criticism. The Pauline authorship
of Hebrews was generally abandoned in critical circles
for the same reasons as once imposed themselves on
Origen's mind, namely, the non-Pauline character of
the language and style of the document. Also the
traditional idea that the writer addressed the Jewish
people as a whole gave way before the distinct evidence
of the Epistle that the recipients were Jewish *Christians*,
and not even Jewish Christians at large but a limited
group, a particular local community known to the writer.
Here critical opinion, sifting out the possible alternatives,
has rallied steadily, though not universally, to the conclusion that the persons addressed in Hebrews were a community of Jewish Christians at *Rome*, Jewish Christians
who formed a section or sept or wing of a Jewish-
Christian congregation or synagogue in that centre. The
main arguments on which the assumption of a Roman
destination for the Epistle are based are the following:

1. There is the reference in xiii. 24 to 'those from

Italy', whose greetings the writer conveys along with his own. While the words 'those from Italy' might be used to describe Christians domiciled in Italy who desired to associate themselves with the writer in a message directed to brethren in some other country, they admit equally well of the interpretation that the persons in question were Italian Christians, absent from their country, who wished to be remembered to their friends at home.

2. There is the fact that the first traces of the existence of the Epistle are at Rome, where substantial extracts from its language occur, as has been noted, in the First Epistle of Clement,[1] and where occasional, though less distinct, echoes of its ideas can be detected, a generation later, in the Visions and Similitudes of Hermas.

3. There are the allusions in the Epistle to the impressive past history of the community addressed, the beneficence of its service to the saints (vi. 10), the conspicuous fidelity of its behaviour under the ordeal of public prosecution (x. 32-34), and the eminence of its former leaders (xiii. 7). All these, if Italy be taken to represent the general direction in which we are to look, would point with force to the Church at Rome as the likeliest particular centre in which to find the community located. It may be remembered that the experience of suffering and persecution has a marked prominence in St. Paul's Epistle to the Church at Rome.[2] Persecution was a condition of existence with which the latter was apparently familiar.

4. There is the notable absence, both in Hebrews and Romans, of all reference to Gnostic and heathen

---

[1] 1 Clement xxxvi. 1-5, lxi. 3, lxiv. 1.
[2] Romans v. 3-5, viii. 18-19, 31-39.

errors on the part of the Christians counselled. The only erroneous teaching which is commented upon in Hebrews concerns food-laws, and this is a point in curious agreement with St. Paul's Romans, where the same or similar doctrines are attributed to a section of the Roman community, and form the only subject on which the Apostle takes the community seriously to task.[1] Again, the call 'not to forsake the gathering of yourselves together' in Hebrews (x. 24-25) has a very close inverse parallel in St. Paul's injunction to the Roman brethren to 'accept' or 'welcome' one another.[2] These coincidences, to mention no others, constitute a strong case for taking the two Epistles together as dual witnesses to the character of Roman Christianity. No ethnic aberrations in this metropolitan Church, only minority tendencies towards Jewish practices! For the freedom of the same Church from the infection of pagan syncretism Dr. E. F. Scott appositely quotes a later eulogy which represents the Roman Christians as 'filtered clean from every foreign stain'.[3]

The older theory, then, accepting on good grounds the Roman destination of the Epistle, goes on to interpret the situation in Hebrews by assuming the existence in the Roman-Christian community of a group of Jewish Christians who were drifting from their Christian moorings back to Judaism, and whom the writer warns. This is a more debatable position. In favour of the theory of a reversion to Judaism, stress has been laid on a number of factors in the contemporary history of the Church and of the Empire. These include:

(*a*) Christian disappointment over the non-fulfilment

---

[1] Romans xiv. 13-23.   [2] Romans xv. 7.
[3] Ignatius, Letter to the Romans, Preface; E. F. Scott, *The Epistle to the Hebrews*, p. 13.

of the expectation of the Lord's return (x. 35-38);

(b) the growing pressure of persecution, or of social opinion adverse to the confessors of Christ (x. 32-34);

(c) the increasing strength of Jewish propaganda at Rome under the Flavian emperors—this frankly presupposes a post-Neronian dating for the Epistle; and

(d) the sentimental revulsion produced in Jewish hearts by the political extinction of Jerusalem and the cessation of the Temple-worship—this again posits a date later than the year A.D. 70.

It has been argued that these last events, or pre-monitions of them, may have had the effect in certain circles of creating an archaising tendency of thought in the direction of the ancient Biblical records of the 'Tabernacle' and the cultus. It has even been supposed that the passage, Hebrews vi. 4-6, which denies the possibility of a second 'repentance', is expressly pointed against persons who, disappointed with Christianity, were seeking to re-ignite the flickering lamp of religion at the altar-fires, so to speak, of the old religion. Such reversion the writer pronounces to be 'an impossibility'. It is not only not a renovation of repentance, but a re-crucifixion of the Son of God.[1]

But, over and above the fact that this is rather a strained interpretation to put on the word 'repentance' in the passage in question, it has to be observed that only the first and second of the above factors can be admitted, on the evidence of Hebrews itself, to have been operative in the minds and lives of the group of

[1] See Dr. A. Nairne, *The Epistle of Priesthood*, pp. 13-15.

Christians indicated in the letter. There is not an atom of evidence that either the third or the fourth entered as elements into the situation. In other words, *any dangers which made themselves felt from the side of Judaism were not of a racial, or political, or sentimental, but of a purely religious kind*.

Granting, however, that deflecting influences of a religious kind were at work on the community from the side of Judaism, we do not necessarily conclude that the peril was that of a conscious and deliberate return to Judaism. Such an inference overruns the evidence, and prejudges the question of the historical bearings of the Epistle. The latter does not actually speak of apostasy to Judaism. It does speak of apostasy from the living God. This implies certainly a falling away from the truth of Christianity, but it leaves the door open to other interpretations of the group's unfaithfulness besides that of a return by choice to the old religion. The delinquents may have been Christians who had no thought of abandoning the Christian position, but who, nevertheless, were hanging back from accepting the full consequences of their calling, were not maintaining their original 'confidence' in it, were certainly not going forward to 'perfection'. This, it would seem, is as much as the Epistle itself warrants us in holding with regard to the motives actuating the community. It would appear, therefore, that the traditional explanation of the position of the 'Hebrews' at Rome leaves something to be desired.

While strong reasons remain, as we shall see, for upholding the Jewish-Christian character of the group, it is possible that the danger to their faith lay not in a return to Judaism as such, but in a retardation of their Christian progress by factors having their causes in the

Jewish element in their Christianity, in other words, by an undue assertion of their Jewish-Christian inheritance.

THE MODERN VOLTE-FACE IN CRITICISM

The modern theory, in seeking an explanation of Hebrews, detaches the Epistle altogether from its traditional Jewish-Christian moorings and floats it out into the mid-stream of the general life of the contemporary Church. This change of front dates back at least to 1836, when E. M. Röth published at Frankfurt a work designed to show that 'the Epistle commonly styled to the Hebrews was intended for Christians of Gentile extraction (*ad Christianos genere gentiles*)'.

According to this view, the danger of the group was not that of reaction towards Judaism but either of falling away to unbelief or disappointment with religion generally—so we are asked to understand the language of Hebrews vi. 3-6—or, alternatively, of succumbing to the fascinations of Hellenistic paganism, mystery-cults, angel-worship, theosophy, and the like. The purpose of the letter on this showing was to assert the finality and grandeur of the Christian religion, to emphasise its incomparable greatness with respect to other faiths, to insist on its absoluteness as a redemption-mystery. Here let full acknowledgment be made of the stimulus given to modern studies in this field by H. von Soden who stated the new theory fully in his edition of the Epistle in 1890, by Weizsäcker, Jülicher, McGiffert and other scholars who gave the theory publicity with varying emphasis on this or that point in the argument, and more recently by James Moffatt and E. F. Scott who have popularised the new approach to Hebrews by their lucid and attractive powers of exposition. Dr. Moffatt's *Commentary on the Epistle to the Hebrews* (1924) is the most valuable critical study of the book which the modern age has received. It draws upon very rich knowledge of the Wisdom-literature of Judaism, of the voluminous writings of Philo of Alexandria, and of the religious and ethical philosophy of the contemporary Hellenistic world, and it is lit up by fresh, sympathetic, and incisive exegetical insight. Dr. Scott also in various books, notably *The Epistle to the Hebrews: its Doctrine and significance* (1922), has contributed very greatly to the modern re-awakening of a lively interest in the Epistle, and has stated the new critical theory in a very fascinating way. Nevertheless, great as is the debt which we owe to these scholars for research and acumen which have gone far to advance our general understanding of the Epistle, I find it impossible to think that the critical theory to which their support has been given and their insights annexed marks a step in the right direction.

The arguments which they have adduced in favour of the position do not, as I consider, establish the full conclusions which they have thought to build upon them. For one thing, these arguments start to a considerable extent from *a priori* assumptions with regard to Christian history in the apostolic age: the influence of St. Paul, for instance, is given an inordinate importance with regard to contemporary Christian teaching in the World-Church. For another thing, they take off, not from the central substance of the doctrine of the Epistle but from peripheral features, and it is difficult, therefore, to think that the conclusions at which these scholars arrive represent a real landing on historical ground. In defence of this criticism it is only

B

necessary to call the witness of the reasons which are ordinarily offered in support of the position.

CRITICISM OF THE MODERN THEORY

According to Dr. Moffatt, 'Hebrews' is a misleading name for the book, for whether as an equivalent for Jewish Christians or for Hebrew-speaking Jewish Christians, the title is 'inapplicable to the circle for whom this remarkable treatise was produced'.

1. Importance is attached to the absence from Hebrews of all reference to 'the distinction of Jew and Gentile' in the Church, to the non-occurrence of even the terms Jew and Gentile, and to the omission of all allusion to such matters as circumcision, the authority of the Law with relation to Christians, and the antithesis of faith and works. It is argued that these omissions point to a time when the issues in question had ceased to have a living significance for religion, and therefore indicate a society which was no longer distinctively either Jewish-Christian or Gentile-Christian in consciousness, but already incipiently Catholic.

To this it may be replied that all these omissions admit of being perfectly well explained if we suppose the writer of the Epistle to have been addressing a group of Christians of Jewish extraction or tradition, who formed a self-contained, self-conscious religious unit within the larger Church. Such a society would not in principle be interested in, or affected by any of the controversies turning on the distinction of Jew and Gentile. These would not ordinarily come within the horizon of a Jewish-Christian group's particular consciousness, nor would it be necessary for a group-leader to introduce or argue about them. The absence from

Hebrews of the above features, therefore, is no sign that the Epistle had not Jewish Christians as its objective.

2. It is contended, rather paradoxically, that the pre-occupation of the Epistle with the Old Testament priesthood and cultus, so far from indicating or proving the Jewish-Christian character of the community, does the exact opposite. For (i) Judaism at this time, it is contended, 'was not a matter of ritual but of fidelity to the Law', and (ii) the Jewish ordinances and the cultus were not living issues in Christianity after the time of St. Paul, least of all in cosmopolitan Rome.[1]

Here it has to be insisted by way of answer that what was true regarding contemporary Judaism was not necessarily true of *Jewish Christianity* when we allow for the renovation of religious insight and Biblical interest which had come to it through Christ;[2] and to say that after St. Paul Christianity had ceased to give any thought to the Old Testament cultus and ritual is to give to St. Paul's particular concentration on the purely ethical aspect of the Law an unwarrantable authority for Churches lying outside the domain of his personal activity. It is to make Paulinism the complete measure and standard of Christian belief in the world-wide Church. It fails to allow for the personal equation in the matter of St. Paul's peculiar emphases in his doctrine of grace. St. Paul had done a great work in Galatia, at Corinth, in Asia and elsewhere. But he was one who from early days had brooded over the Law in its aspect of *moral demand*, and for whom the question of questions was and remained how to be

[1] So E. F. Scott, *The Epistle to the Hebrews*, p. 17 etc.; J. Moffatt, *Commentary*, p. xvi etc.
[2] Cf. Luke xxiv. 32 etc.

right with God in the face of that demand, how to be personally delivered from inward contradiction and frustration—the law of sin in his members as he calls it—how to attain to 'no condemnation' and 'peace'. St. Paul's doctrine of grace had thus acquired a highly individualised expression.

But this does not exclude the possibility that there were other Jewish Christians who had come to the heart of the Christian revelation of grace along another route, parallel indeed but separate. The writer to the Hebrews may have been one of these. He may not, like Saul of Tarsus, have brooded over the script of the moral Law in solitude, but there is nothing to disprove that he had stood, actually or in spirit, with the hushed assemblies which witnessed the offering of the sacrifices for sin in the Temple, or had been present when the high-priest made his oblation on the Day of Atonement. Nor is there anything to exclude the assumption that the supreme question for him was and remained how to be 'clean' from the guilt of sin, how to be 'sanctified' and 'perfected' for approach to God. If we allow the possibility of this, and assume that the *ritual approach* to the understanding of the Christian redemption—in the doctrine of Christ as our great High-Priest, whose self-oblation fulfils the Jewish cultus—may have been of the very essence of the matter for this Jewish-Christian theologian, and would ordinarily be propagated by him in his teaching, then, though we cannot say on this ground alone that the group which he addressed in the Epistle was necessarily Jewish-Christian, we cannot refuse to admit the possibility that it was. For he would teach his doctrine everywhere and, like St. Paul, to the Jew first.

3. It is insisted that the great use of the Old Testa-

ment made by the writer, whose version was the Septuagint which he knew chiefly in the A text form, lends no colour at all to the assumption that the persons he addressed were Jewish Christians. No more, for that part, it is said, do his archaising tendencies, his dwelling on Israel's experience in the desert, his interest in the Tabernacle and in its furnishings, and his fondness for ritual details in his allusions to the cultus. The Septuagint, we are reminded, was the Bible of the whole Church, from which Apostles and others opened up the mystery of redemption for all Christians, Gentile as well as Jewish. St. Paul in writing to the Galatian and Corinthian Churches, which were predominantly Gentile-Christian, makes a similar use of the Old Testament as his text-book, and so later do Clement of Rome, the Apologists such as Justin Martyr, and others in writing to the world. The extensive employment of Biblical types and allegories, therefore, proves nothing, it is contended, with reference to the character of the community which the writer to the Hebrews has in mind.

To this it may be replied that, if the writer's extensive use of Old Testament material does not prove the Jewish-Christian character of the group receiving the letter, neither does it prove that the group was Gentile-Christian or Catholic. It must also be considered that, if the writer were taking his stand on the Old Testament merely in order to oppose some general Christian drift to irreligion or to paganism, it would have been open to him to go other ways about the matter than by leading an elaborate proof that Jesus is our High-Priest after the order of Melchizedek. What needs to be explained in Hebrews is not the writer's choice of the Old Testament as his starting-point and quarry of theological argument, but the nature of the particular argument which he proceeds to draw out of it.

If, as is alleged by some defenders of the modern theory of Hebrews, a Jewish-Christian group would not, as such, be particularly interested in reasonings based on the Jewish high-priesthood and the ritual, much less would a Gentile-Christian or Catholic-Christian group be likely to be so interested, especially as, in turning from Christianity, such persons would be turning also from its holy Books. Moreover, the Septuagint has a very great deal to say about unbelief, the folly of thinking that 'there is no God', and it has a great deal to say also about the gods of paganism and the wickedness of sacrifices and offerings to demons, and if the writer to the Hebrews were calling attention to its teaching in order to warn a Gentile-born or Catholic section of the Church against a side-slip to unbelief or heathenism, he could have started from this more broadly relevant Old Testament material, and left Melchizedek and Psalm cx. alone. But there is not a word in Hebrews about unbelief in the sense of irreligion pure and simple, nor about pagan rites and mysteries, nor about the tables and cups of demons. Neither, for that part, is anything heard of these ethnic perils in the other great New Testament document addressed to the Roman Christians, St. Paul's Epistle to the Romans. In other Pauline letters, and very markedly in Galatians, 1 Corinthians, and Colossians, which were all addressed to Churches in the Eastern half of the Mediterranean world, we find regular allusion to the beliefs, the practices, and the moral aberrations of Hellenistic society. In Hebrews and in Romans, on the other hand, the argument for the Christian religion is presented consistently and exclusively in terms of its relation to

Judaism. This is a feature of some interest in these Epistles which has not been sufficiently noticed in modern works whether on Hebrews or on Romans.

For these and other reasons which will be brought out in the course of the succeeding chapters, neither the older nor the more recent approach to the Epistle can be regarded as satisfactory. Neither of them has brought the situation behind the Epistle into full and clear historical focus, and to this extent neither has done adequate justice to the theological and practical meaning of Hebrews. There is some justification, therefore, for attempting a reconsideration of the problem in some of its aspects, and igniting a fresh spark to explore the way.

PROVISIONAL STATEMENT OF POSITIONS ADVANCED IN THE PRESENT WORK

In what follows we shall be engaged in the task of seeking a fresh integration of Hebrews into the historical development of Early Christian thought and life. The first problem will concern the relation in which the eschatology and Christological doctrine of the Epistle stand to the gospel of the world-mission of Christianity. We shall inquire into the character of the Roman-Christian community as a whole and into the position within that community of the particular minority of Christians to whom Hebrews was written. In the course of the succeeding chapters I shall offer reasons in defence of the following, among other, positions:

I. The key to the Epistle is only to be found by examining the history of the world-mission of Christianity from its inception in the work of Stephen.

II. The direction and tone of the writer's thought are to be explained by his concentration of mind on the critical significance of the moment marked by the entrance of Christ into time. In Christ the Eternal World has announced itself, throwing all past religious history into the shadow, putting an end to the Law and the Cultus of Israel, and leaving no place in Christianity for Jewish-Christian archaising.

III. The particular message of the Epistle, that with the Priesthood and Oblation of Christ the Jewish means of grace are ended, represents the elaboration of a fundamental and integral element in the theology of the world-mission of Christianity. While St. Paul gives us a great part of that world-mission theology, he gives us only a part.

IV. The community of Christians established at Rome by the world-mission was predominantly Jewish-Christian in composition and character, rather than Gentile-Christian. Separatist tendencies within that Church inclined to the Jewish rather than to the Gnostic or Hellenistic side. The minority group to which Hebrews was addressed was definitely Jewish-Christian.

V. The sin of the 'Hebrews' group was not that of abandoning Christianity for Judaism, but rather of remaining as Christians under the covert of the Jewish religion, living too much in the Jewish part of their Christianity, and so missing the true horizon of the eschatological calling.

CHAPTER II

STEPHEN AND THE WORLD-MISSION
OF CHRISTIANITY

THE Acts of the Apostles states that the world-mission
of Christianity was already announced to the Apostles
in and with the Easter experiences of the first Christian
days. The historian records that among the numinous
events, visions, auditions, and other phenomena of that
extraordinary time there came as the climax and end
of the revelations the intimation of the Lord to His
Apostles that they would be His witnesses in Judea and
Samaria and to the ends of the earth.[1] It is interesting,
however, that, on the showing of the same authority,
this disclosure was made only after a certain question
which was trembling on the lips of the Twelve had been
propounded and virtually dismissed:

'Lord, is it at this time that You restore the Kingdom
to Israel?'[2]

In the actual order of things, the inception of the world-
mission of Christianity dates from events which had
their origin in the work of Stephen; and between the
Galileans with *their* outlook on history, and the proto-
martyr with his, there entered as middle-term the
Pentecostal baptism of the Church.

There is general agreement that the record of the
opening chapters of Acts is, for the most part, based on
a Jerusalem source or incorporates material amassed

[1] Acts i. 8.   [2] Acts i. 6 f.

by the compiler of Acts in Jerusalem and Judea. While there is some idealising of the events of the first days of the Church by the Gentile-Christian historian who, visiting Palestine and the Holy City a generation after those events, came under the powerful spell of the Mother-Church and of the Christian tradition which he found there, there is no reason to question the substantial truth of his general representation of the early days, especially in the point of the pre-occupation of the original disciples with the thought of the Lord's immediate return to set up a Kingdom in Zion.

With this pre-occupation it is possible to connect another feature in the Acts representation, which need not at all be due to idealisation, namely, the clinging of the first Galilean group of disciples to the Temple and to the Jewish ordinances. While the community had its private gatherings for instruction by the Apostles and 'the common life', and for 'the breaking of the bread' and the prayers,[1] the public activities of the Apostles were carried on in the Temple precincts, to which the Church and the crowds resorted.[2] Nor is this assiduous frequenting of the Holy Place to be set down merely to that quickening of religious life and zeal which had come to the Church through the events of the post-Resurrection days. Was there not a word of sacred prophecy in their ears which seemed to connect the Messiah's return with the glory of the Sanctuary and the honouring of the ordinances of worship?

'Look! I send My Messenger to prepare the way for Me, and the Lord whom you seek will come suddenly to His temple.'[3]

---

[1] Acts ii. 42, 45, 46b, iv. 23 f., v. 42.
[2] Acts ii. 46a, iii. 1-3, 11 ff., v. 12, 20-21, 25, 42.
[3] Malachi iii. 1.

The passage is from Malachi, and the whole book of Malachi should be read for the intimate connection subsisting in the prophet's thought between the divine salvation and the right ordering of the cultus. But if prophetic expectations of this kind kept the original 'Kingdom-to-Israel' community in close adhesion to the Temple and the Jewish ordinances, it is another outlook which confronts us when we turn to Stephen and his theology in chapters vi.-vii. of Acts.

STEPHEN

The narrative of Acts vi.-vii. rests undoubtedly on an ancient source, and embodies traditions of the origins of the world-mission of Christianity which had been preserved at Caesarea or at Antioch. Features of the record, above all, the sermon of Stephen in chapter vii. with its rugged and angular style and phrasing, and the difficulty of fitting its substance neatly into the adjoining context, point to the derivation of the material from a written document of some kind, and impart to this section of Acts a very great historical value. The narrative opens at a point when, with the introduction into the growing Church of large numbers of 'Hellenists', that is, of Jews of Diaspora birth or outlook, who had been converted to the Christian faith at Jerusalem, a remonstrance was addressed to the other section of the community, consisting of the Galilean Apostles and their adherents, that the Hellenist widows were neglected in the daily grant of relief from the common funds. The language of Acts at this point is significant: the complaint of the Hellenists is directed 'to the Hebrews'.[1] It is possible that the grievance in

---

[1] Acts vi. 1.

question was only the symptom of a larger tension between the two groups, arising from broad differences of outlook and sympathy. In any case, the machinery for the administration of the social life of the community had broken down, and seven men, commended by their possession of the Holy Spirit and wisdom, were, according to Acts, elected by the Church and consecrated by the Apostles to meet the requirements of the new situation.

These seven men bear Hellenist names, and Stephen at once, and Philip a little later, are found exercising not merely an administrative but an evangelistic function. Stephen comes to the front as a man 'full of faith and the Holy Spirit', 'full of grace and power', whose work is attended by every kind of numinous manifestation, 'great wonders and signs', as the Acts reports.[1] Then comes a crisis. Stephen's teaching arouses the vehement hostility of a section of the Jewish community who, as their derivation from the Jerusalem synagogues listed in the Acts narrative—Roman, North African, Cilician and Asian—shows, were obviously Hellenistic or Diaspora Jews. Failing to make headway by argument against their formidable antagonist, these former co-religionists of Stephen instigate legal proceedings against him.

The charges formulated against Stephen in Acts vi. are interesting. For the first time in the Acts narrative we hear of a breach occurring *within* Christianity between the gospel on the one hand and the Temple and the Law on the other. Stephen is accused of blasphemy 'against Moses and God'.[2] We have to make the usual allowance here for the tendency inseparable from *ex parte* statements to exaggerate and distort the truth.

[1] Acts vi. 8.   [2] Acts vi. 11.

There can be little doubt, however, that some kind of
historical foundation underlies the terms of the indictment put forward by the suborned witnesses.

> 'This man never stops talking against this holy
> place and the Law.'
> 'We have heard him saying that this Jesus the
> Nazarene means to do away with this place and
> to alter the customs which Moses handed down
> to us.' [1]

What, then, do these allegations actually imply on
Stephen's side? That he, as a Diaspora Jew, was anti-
pathetic by temperament or religious theory to the
Temple, the cultus, the whole ritual element in religion
as such? That is not asserted in the narrative, and it
is not necessarily true. There were Diaspora Jews who,
in presenting their religion to the Gentile world, turned
the cloak of the Law inside out, exhibiting and stressing
its inward and prophetic lining, its spiritual and ethical
part, rather than its exterior of ritual requirement. In
the interests of such propaganda, for instance, certain
Greek iambic verses were interpolated by Jewish
apologists into copies of more than one Greek dramatist.
They are quoted by Pseudo-Justin,[2] and with some
variations by Clement of Alexandria.[3] The former
ascribes them to Philemon, the latter to Menander.
An extract from the Greek text is given by Schürer,[4]
of which a translation may be here offered.

> Dost think by offerings, thy sin to hide,
> Thou bring'st, O man, the Godhead to thy side?

---

[1] Acts vi. 13-14.   [2] *De Monarchia*, 4.
[3] *Stromateis*, V. 14.
[4] *Geschichte des Jüdischen Volkes*, 4th ed. (1909), Bd. III, p. 137,
note 4.

Astray thou art, and foolish is thy thought,
For man to God by goodness must be brought.
Thy soul must answer to the measuring rod,
Justice alone is sacrifice to God.

But that an animus against the cultus *per se* was characteristic of the Hellenist Jews in general is too much to assume, and is disproved by the storm of indignation which Stephen's reputed blasphemy provoked in the Hellenist synagogues at Jerusalem; and that it does not supply the key to Stephen's personal position is shown by the terms in which in his apologia he speaks of the sacrifices and the Tabernacle themselves. Discoursing of Israel in the wilderness-period, Stephen avers that 'God abandoned them to worship the heavenly host', the star-gods or angels, that is, to whom the pagan nations were subject, and then he quotes the prophet Amos:

'Did you offer victims and sacrifices to Me, these
    forty years in the desert, O House of Israel?
Nay, what you lifted up was Moloch's tent, and the
    star of your god Rephan—simulacra which you
    made to worship!'

In other words, what Amos meant, according to Stephen, was not that God had not commanded sacrifices and oblations, but that Israel had diverted its offerings and its sanctuary to idolatrous purposes. We have thus to look for another explanation of Stephen's attitude to the cultus and the Law.

THE ESCHATOLOGY OF STEPHEN

That explanation comes to light, I think, when we study carefully Stephen's apologia, his great review of Israel's religious history which is given in the seventh

chapter of Acts. At the close of that remarkable discourse, we are told that the dying martyr, fixing his
eyes on heaven, saw the 'glory of God', and Jesus
standing at the right hand of God, and cried:

'Look! I see heaven open, and the Son of Man
standing at God's right hand.' [1]

Stephen's direction of mind towards the Ultimate
Event in the revelation of God in Christ appears here
with extraordinary vividness, and it is impossible not
to ask whether in this direction of mind, ordinarily
called eschatology, we have not the true key to his
characteristic work and witness and to much else that
follows in the history of the world-mission of Christianity.

The words just quoted represent the only instance in
the New Testament of the apocalyptic title 'Son of
Man' being found on any lips but those of Jesus.
This remarkable fact is not one to be undervalued or
ignored. It is, on the face of it, a very distinct piece
of evidence that, actually and historically, *Stephen
grasped and asserted the more-than-Jewish-Messianic
sense in which the office and significance of Jesus in
religious history were to be understood*. More clearly
than others, and indeed uniquely in that first age of
Christianity, he perceived the universal range and
bearing of the Christ-event, by which the call of God
had passed from the Jewish people to embrace humanity
at large.

Whereas the Jewish nationalists were holding to the
permanence of their national historical privilege, and
even the 'Hebrew' Christians gathered round the
Apostles were, with all their new Messianic faith,

[1] Acts vii. 56.

idealising the sacred institutions of the past, 'continuing stedfastly in the temple', 'going up to the temple at the hour of prayer' which was also the hour of the sacrificial service, sheltering under the eaves of the Holy Place, Stephen saw that the Messiah was on the throne of the Universe.

The Son of Man, spoken of by Daniel the prophet, had arrived in the presence of God, and had received from God 'dominion, and glory, and a kingdom, that all peoples, nations, and languages should serve him'.[1] In seeing this, did Stephen also see, at the same moment, that the Temple-worship, the sacrifices, the Law, all the holy institutions of the past, were thereby transcended and antiquated, and that *the call to the Church of Jesus was to leave the Temple and all that went with it behind, and to go forward*, no longer clinging to historical securities, no longer thinking to capitalise the grace of God in the Jewish ordinances and cultus, but throwing in its lot with the crucified Son of Man, to whom the throne of the world and the Lordship of the Age to Come belonged? With this there must go another question.

All the Apostles and their followers were eschatologists. All of them, that is to say, were looking for the advent of the Lord from heaven. All were seeing in that event the Ultimate Event of time, the one thing which would give meaning to history and consummate the Divine salvation. But whereas the original Apostles and witnesses thought that Jesus would come back to *them*,—'Lord, is it at this time that You restore the Kingdom to Israel?'—*did Stephen say that they must go out and, so to speak, anticipate the Son of Man's coming by proclaiming Him to every nation and people*

[1] Daniel vii. 13-14.

of that larger world which was now included in His dominion?

These are questions that demand an answer, and the answers, of course, can only be sought in what is recorded of Stephen's own philosophy of history. When, however, we turn to his apologia with its trenchant and remorseless indictment of Israel's resistance to God in the past, we find the whole record to be indeed dominated by the sense of an Ultimate End towards which God has been ever seeking to lead and impel His people. 'The God of glory appeared to our father Abraham . . . and said to him Go out!' 'After the death of his father, God transported him into this land in which you now dwell.'[1] As long, however, as Abraham lived, he was only a wanderer, a landless *ger* in a country of promise.[2] So it was with Abraham's posterity, Isaac, Jacob, and the patriarchs, so it was with Joseph and Moses.[3] When the theophany came to Moses at the bush, it laid on him the command to 'lead forth' the people of God from Egypt.[4]

Now, however, begins the contradiction, the great unbelief of the people of God. All the patriarchs were itinerants, pilgrims, sojourners, seekers of a land of promise. Now comes the harking back to Egypt and the past, the resistance to God's word and Spirit.[5] Israel rejects Moses, the prototype and prophet of the Christ, who had received the 'living oracles' to give to it. Israel had in the desert the 'tent' or tabernacle of witness, fashioned after a revealed 'pattern'. This tent was brought into Canaan, and transmitted and maintained by 'Joshua' and the fathers. In its mobile character—so we may here fill out the interstices of the

---

[1] Acts vii. 4.　　[2] Acts vii. 5.　　[3] Acts vii. 6-21.
[4] Acts vii. 22-36.　　　　[5] Acts vii. 37-43.

C

argument—the tent was a type or figure of God's never-ceasing, never-halted appointments for His people's salvation. But the time came when Israel under David desired a more stable and permanent dwelling for the Most High, and Solomon built Him a 'house'.

At this point Stephen's indignation at the situation confronting him on the side of his Jewish antagonists flares up, and quoting Solomon's words at the dedication of the Temple, he exclaims:

'The Most High does not dwell in temples made by hands. Heaven is My throne, and earth a footstool for My feet! What house will you build for Me, saith the Lord, or what is the place of My rest?' [1]

The point is that the Temple was not intended, any more than the Tabernacle, to become a *permanent* institution, halting the advance of the divine plan for the people of God. Turning, therefore, upon his unbelieving audience, Stephen cries: 'You always resist the Holy Spirit. . . . You received the Law in charges given by the angels, and you have not observed it.' [2]

It is plain that Stephen's passionate outburst at this point is not against Solomon's act in itself, for he quotes Solomon's words in defence of his own thesis. His indignation is rather at the blindness of the Jewish people at this time of crisis, at the failure of his opponents to see that with the coming of the Messiah the hour had struck for *moving on* from the Temple and the Jewish institutions. The revelation given in the Law had been superseded. Its glory had been swallowed up in a higher glory.

It has been represented—and vii. 52, with the connection which is there established between Israel's

<hr>

[1] Acts vii. 48-49.   [2] Acts vii. 51, 53.

persecution of the prophets in the past and the betrayal and murder of Jesus in the present, lends some colour to the idea—that the central theme of Stephen's retrospect of history is that Israel has consistently and in every age opposed the saviours sent to it from God, and this opposition has culminated in the crucifixion of Jesus. But clearer and more consonant with the whole tenor of the discourse is the interpretation that what Israel has resisted is the supra-historical purpose which God has had for His chosen people. This purpose has been made evident at every stage of bygone religious life, and it has been ever directed to the carrying of the nation outwards and onwards to a final goal, an End not to be confused or identified with any past or present stage of religious history. Resistance to this supra-historical purpose has been the radical cause of Israel's rejection of the Lord's messengers. *Israel has been tempted to identify its salvation with historical and earthly securities and fixtures, and Stephen cannot but see the same danger in the attitude of the 'Hebrew' brethren in the Church.* His words are indeed to the Jews, but his animadversions on Moses and the Law, and on the Holy Place and the Tradition, could not but have oblique reference to the conservatism of a section of the Christian community.

Here, then, we have one most essential feature of the eschatology of Stephen. Let it be repeated that Stephen's emphasis on the Tabernacle or tent of the early days rather than on the Temple—a feature which the Epistle to the Hebrews shares in a marked degree— belongs to the very substance of his representation of religious history. *The mobile sanctuary of the early days corresponds with the idea of the ever-onward call of God to His people, the static temple does not.* But there is more than this one feature to justify us at this point in bringing the teaching of Stephen into close comparison with that of the Epistle to the Hebrews.

THE APOLOGIA OF STEPHEN AND THE EPISTLE TO THE HEBREWS

So many of the emphases in these Stephen-chapters of Acts repeat themselves in the Epistle! We note:

(a) the attitude of Stephen to the Cultus and Law of Judaism;

(b) his declaration that Jesus means to change and supersede these things;

(c) his sense of the divine call to the people of God being a call to 'Go out';

(d) his stress on the ever-shifting scene in Israel's life, and on the ever-renewed homelessness of the faithful;

(e) his thought of God's Word as 'living';

(f) his incidental allusion to Joshua in connection with the promise of God's 'Rest';

(g) his idea of the 'angels' being the ordainers of God's Law;

(h) his directing of his eyes to Heaven and to Jesus.

All these are elements which recur in the Epistle to the Hebrews, and the question at once arises whether Stephen's passionate concentration of mind on the eschatological nature of the Christian calling does not —through the medium of the world-mission—provide the real starting-point from which to seek an understanding of the specific message of Hebrews. Before, however, this inquiry is undertaken, it is necessary to trace a little further the historical consequences of Stephen's challenge to the Church of his time.

THE RISE OF THE CHRISTIAN WORLD-MISSION

Stephen's manifesto, while primarily an attack on the unbelieving Jews, brought with it as a real though indirect consequence the shattering of the complacency of the original Jerusalem Church. It created a division in the ranks of that Church. It confirmed the conservative 'Hebrew' Christians—absorbed, all of them, in traditional ideas of the Lord's coming—in their attitude of passive waiting where they were. While the Jewish-Hellenist leaders who adhered to the martyr were 'scattered', and went out to preach the gospel, not only under the compulsion of persecution but in fidelity to Stephen's teaching, the Hebrew-Christian Apostles remained at Jerusalem,[1] within the covert of the Temple and the ordinances. The statement in Acts at this point probably reports only the action of the heads of the two parties, leaving the fortunes of their humbler followers undetermined. In course of time, when St. Peter, and possibly other Apostles, were constrained to move out and to take part in the wider mission inaugurated by Stephen's men, stricter, older-fashioned Christians grouped themselves around James of Jerusalem, and James was a pattern-saint of the legal and Levitical type.

The flying remnants of Stephen's party began the world-mission of Christianity first in Judea, and then in Samaria and the towns on the coast.[2] Here Philip was the leading spirit, and concurrent with his activities was the persecuting campaign carried on by a Rabbinical Jew, the young Saul of Tarsus.[3] An extension of the mission of Stephen's followers presently took them as

[1] Acts viii. 1.   [2] Acts viii. 4-40.
[3] Acts viii. 2-3, ix. 1 ff.

far as Phoenicia and Cyprus—here undoubtedly we are following an Antiochian source-narrative of Acts—and up to this point the method of the agents had restricted their evangelism to Jews in the various areas. At Antioch, however, to which they next moved on, a section of the missionaries—Hellenist-Jewish Christians of Cyprus and Cyrene—addressed themselves to Greeks: such at least would seem to be the right understanding of the textually dubious passage, Acts xi. 20. The response was a very remarkable one, and now there appears on the scene a new convert, the most notable figure to be swept into the current of the world-mission. This was Saul of Tarsus, the very Saul who had carried on a persecuting crusade against the Church. Brought by Barnabas to Antioch, Saul quickly took his place with Barnabas at the head of the mission in that centre. In his teaching the great antithesis between the gospel and Judaism, which Stephen had formulated, became particularly pointed against the Law as a rule of moral observance rather than against the cultus, for in Saul's case, as has been noted,[1] the Law as the embodiment of the divine moral imperative had played the dominant part in his soul's experience of God. This fact was destined to impart a distinctive accent to St. Paul's interpretation of the gospel within the sphere of the world-mission.

It can hardly be doubted that centrifugal forces of the same kind as had carried the gospel to Antioch took it also by the hands of other followers of Stephen to other world-centres. Here unfortunately we no longer have the solid ground of the Acts narrative beneath our feet to support us, but it is scarcely possible that the message of Christianity was not brought about this

[1] See above, pp. 19 f.

time to Alexandria with its teeming Jewish-Hellenist population and its intimate connections with Jerusalem. The fact of such contact seems, indeed, to be indicated by the frequency in Acts itself of incidental references to Egypt, Libya, Cyrene, and Alexandria.[1] In any case, some explanation is needed of the knowledge of Christianity acquired about this period by an Alexandrian Jew of the name of Apollos, and possibly by another Alexandrian Jew who later was to write the Epistle to the Hebrews. The vagueness of the institution of Apollos in Christianity [2] may indicate that an organised Church had not been formed at Alexandria before the time of his leaving that city, but that his was a soul attracted and drawn in by the current of the world-mission there seems no good reason to question. We have also to explain the rise about this time of a Christian community at Rome. It is possible that here, as at Alexandria, no fully organised Church was founded at the beginning. The converts continued to be attached to the Jewish synagogue. Even as late as the close of the sixth Christian decade no fuller order may have been taken for the distinct life of the community, for St. Paul nowhere in his Epistle to the Romans (except in chapter xvi., which cannot with certainty be accepted as originally belonging to that Epistle) makes use of the word Church, and it is even conceivable that some provision for the supplementing of this deficiency was in the Apostle's mind when he wrote the words of Romans i. 11-13. The Christian community at Rome may still have passed for a Jewish 'sect': cf. Acts xxviii. 22. But whatever the facts may have been as regards the organisation of Christian life at Alexandria and Rome, the hypothesis of the 'going out' of Stephen's

[1] Acts ii. 10, vi. 9, xviii. 24-25.   [2] Acts xviii. 24-26.

followers to these two great world-centres, though there is no record of it in Acts, would satisfactorily account for the beginnings of that life.

It is true that a widespread later tradition connected the beginnings of Alexandrian Christianity with the activity of John Mark. The most definite statement is a report cited in Eusebius to the effect that 'Mark in Egypt preached the gospel, which he also drew up in writing, and was the first to establish churches in Alexandria itself'.[1] The traditional understanding was that Mark's visit to Egypt took place after his separation from St. Paul and his mission with Barnabas in Cyprus.[2] Neither Clement nor Origen, however, makes any mention of a work of Mark at Alexandria, and in any case the possibility remains that other adherents of the world-mission had preached in that centre, even if they had not founded an organised Church, at an earlier time.

As for Rome, our earliest trace of the existence of Christianity in that capital centre does not go further back than A.D. 49, in which year the Emperor Claudius by an edict ordered the Jews out of the city. There is a reference to this expulsion in Acts xviii. 2 as the event which brought Aquila and Priscilla from Italy to Corinth, where St. Paul joined them in the winter of A.D. 49-50, but the same measure may account for the proceedings taken against that Apostle in the previous autumn by the civil authorities at Philippi [3] and by the Jewish population at Thessalonica and Beroea.[4] The only definite statement which has come down to us with regard to the circumstances under which the

[1] Eusebius, *History*, II. 16. See H. B. Swete's *St. Mark*, pp. xviii ff.
[2] Acts xv. 37-39.
[3] Acts xvi. 20-21.
[4] Acts xvii. 5-7, 13.

Claudian edict was issued is the laconic notice in the Roman writer Suetonius, who says of Claudius:

'Judaeos impulsore Chresto assidue tumultuantes
    Roma expulit.' [1]

If we assume that the name 'Chrestus' here is a garbled form of Christus, the meaning will be that Messianic agitations breaking out among the Jews at Rome had drawn down upon them the unfavourable notice of the public authorities, the guardians of the peace, and Claudius acted accordingly. The Jews were protected by the privilege of *religio licita* so long as they kept the peace, and this privilege they had forfeited by their intra-synagogal disputes. The most plausible explanation of the whole episode is that Christian propaganda had been introduced into the synagogues at Rome and had created considerable ferment.

The time of troubles which followed would, of course, involve the Christian members of the Roman synagogues as the prime instigators of the unrest, and it may be to the events of this period that the writer to the Hebrews later alludes when, speaking of an earlier time in his readers' history, after their first 'enlightenment' or baptism, he recalls that they were publicly subjected to insult and outrage, being stripped of their goods, or required to share the deprivations of others, all which hardships they accepted cheerfully, sympathising with prisoners, knowing that there was reserved for them a great and enduring reward.[2]

---

[1] Suetonius, *Claudius*, XXV.
[2] Hebrews x. 32-34.

Divisive Issues created by the World-Mission of Christianity

The great question which concerns us here, in tracing the early course of the world-mission of Christianity, is to determine to what extent the root-principles of Stephen's teaching, his vision of the supra-historical, eschatological nature of the Christian calling, and his opposition of the gospel to the cultus and Law of Judaism as things which Christ had superseded, would be kept to the front in the preaching of his followers. In particular we have to ask—for consideration of this point can no longer be deferred—*whether there would not be a tendency everywhere in the Jewish division of the Church, now mostly drawn from Jewish-Hellenist circles, to form into two parties*, determined by the respective attitudes taken, under various stresses, to the Mosaic Law and ordinances of the past. That such a cleavage of sympathies did take place in the Churches within the Pauline sector of the world-mission is notorious. At Antioch, in the Churches of Galatia, at Philippi, and at Corinth, parties arose for the Law and against the freedom preached by the Apostle. It will not do to assume offhand that the *whole* of the Jewish section in every Church was for the Law, and that the party for freedom was always Gentile. As in the Church at Jerusalem in Stephen's time, the wedge may well have driven itself into and through the Jewish-Christian section of the Churches. Unless we recognise this possibility, we may be over-simplifying the Christian history of the apostolic age. As it is, the division in the Pauline Churches, though radical, turned primarily on the *Law* in the point of its authority or meaning for Christian life and conduct. The issue owed its sharpness, as we have noticed,[1] to St. Paul's particular and psychological predetermination of religious mind. But the possibility that the *cultus* also would enter as a dividing issue in other Churches, if there was any faithfulness to the terms of Stephen's original protest at Jerusalem, must not be overlooked.

It must be remembered that the Law had a ritual and ceremonial as well as an ethical side, and this, of course, was implicitly recognised and covered by the Pauline theology of the subject. But the ritual and ceremonial part of the Law, in the last resort, ran up into, and was concentrated in the sacrificial cultus at Jerusalem. And Jews who had been accustomed to hear 'Moses' read and preached in the synagogues of the Diaspora Sabbath by Sabbath[2] would not all, when they became Christians, readily feel themselves immediately dispensed from all further obligation to the ritual and the ordinances, or be able to regard these as no longer in any sense binding.

The recommendations urged upon St. Paul by James and the presbyters, on the occasion of his last visit to Jerusalem, are a case in point, and they are of great interest for us. They concerned four Jewish-Christian brethren who had taken a 'vow', and St. Paul was asked—for politic reasons be it admitted—to associate himself with these brethren in the vow, to share the ritual acts, and to defray the monetary charges required for the completion of their 'purification'. The requirements included punctilious fulfilment of the votive obligations, visits to the Temple, ceremonial discharge from the vows, and the offering of a sacrifice for each of the votaries.[3] That St. Paul complied with these requirements shows that the cultus-issue might still, under circumstances, exert its pressure on Jewish

---

[1] See above, pp. 19 f., 38.   [2] Acts xv. 21.   [3] Acts xxi. 20-26.

Christians, even Hellenists, and though that pressure would be less strong in centres remote from Jerusalem and the ancient sanctuary, a certain sentiment of reverence for the cultus may be expected to have preserved itself even there. This would continue at least down to the Fall of Jerusalem and the cessation of the sacrifices in the year 70.

If this is recognised, the green light is given us to go forward to the Epistle to the Hebrews with the possibility in our minds that the teaching of Stephen, with which, as we have seen, the Epistle has so many features in common, is not only the matrix within which the theological ideas elaborated in Hebrews first took shape, but indirectly explains *the existence of a minority in the Roman Church who in reaction from the larger freedom of the world-mission gospel were asserting principles and counter-claims akin to those of the original 'Hebrew' section in the Jerusalem Church.* On this hypothesis the author of Hebrews will have been a fervent upholder of the world-mission gospel, who writes to warn this disaffected group, to whom he is personally known, of the serious dangers attending their position. The group are living in the past, they are holding on to old securities, they are 'neglecting' that divine 'salvation' which now in Christ has entered on its final phase or manifestation. What is at stake, the writer tells them, is nothing less than their 'share' in Christ and in the life of 'the world to come'.

So far, all this is only a possibility, only a hypothesis which has to be tested. But to accept the Epistle to the Hebrews as a document of the world-mission of Christianity, comparable with, though distinct in many features from the Pauline proclamation, opens for us an entrancing vista. We stand at a point where, as we watch the river of Christianity flowing to the sea, we see it forming for itself various courses, parallel to a certain extent and complementary. Two of these channels may be recognised in the Epistle to the Hebrews and in the Pauline literature. Here it will be well to keep before the mind the great constitutive features of the world-mission gospel: first, its concentration on the eschatological, heavenly calling of the Church, a point common to all the derivative theologies, though expressed in different forms; secondly, its proclamation of the transcendence of Jesus over the Law and the sacrificial order of the past, which also is common to all, though defined in variant terms. In St. Paul, for example, we find redemption characteristically expressed in forensic terms of *dikaiosune* or 'rightness with God'. In Hebrews it is in ritual terms of *hagiasmos* or 'purification' for approach to God. In the Johannine literature it is in mystical terms of the eternal 'light', 'life', 'love' which have made themselves known in Jesus. All these terms may be interpreted as so many signal-lights demarcating the various channels along which thought in the Christian mission is streaming out into the world's life.

It remains to notice that some exponents of the modern interpretation of the Epistle to the Hebrews have glanced at the teaching of Stephen, but glanced at it only to turn away. Dr. Moffatt, for example, admitted that the closest approach to Hebrews within the New Testament literature in the matter of its typological method and exegetical freedom in handling the Old Testament was to be found in Stephen's discourse in Acts vii. Nevertheless he held the parallelism to break down at such points as the silence of Hebrews with regard to the crime of the Jews in putting Jesus to death, a charge which Stephen labours and grounds on the age-long obstinacy and—Dr. Moffatt adds—the 'externalism' of Israel.[1] But surely the very close analogy between Stephen's teaching and the doctrine of the Epistle is not essentially damaged by the absence of correspondence at this particular point. Hebrews is addressed not to the Jewish nation but to a community of persons within the Christian Church who, though they need to be reminded of the fundamental truths which Stephen taught and the world-mission proclaims, were not themselves involved in the crime of the Jewish people against Jesus and therefore do not come under the brunt of this part of Stephen's attack. No conclusions are, therefore, to be drawn at this point either as against the dependence of Hebrews on Stephen's general principles or in favour of the non-Jewish extraction of the Christians addressed in the Epistle. Dr. E. F. Scott gives fuller recognition to the importance of Stephen's utterance as a factor in the development of the Gentile-Christian Churches and their theology. He admits that 'ideas . . . uncoloured by Paulinism . . . had come, through Stephen, as a direct heritage from the Church at Jerusalem'.[2] But when Dr. Scott speaks of Stephen's discourse as an 'apparently aimless summary of Old Testament events', it may be thought that he has not fully measured the significance of Stephen for the understanding of our Epistle. He has overlooked the eschatology, the concentration of thought on the transcendent, heavenly end of the religious calling, which is the key at once to Stephen's reading of history and to the theology of the writer to the Hebrews.

[1] *Commentary on Hebrews*, pp. lxii f.
[2] *The Epistle to the Hebrews*, pp. 63-65.

CHAPTER III

THE ADMONITORY SECTIONS OF THE EPISTLE. THE ESCHATOLOGICAL LIFE

In Hebrews we find a series of sections, some short, some long, in which the writer pauses in the course of his didactic argument to address warnings or exhortations to the readers: the letter as a whole is indeed an exhortation or appeal with which they are asked to 'bear' (xiii. 22). These passages are of very great interest as showing how the author envisaged the religious situation of the particular society to which he was writing. They open windows on that situation, and to this extent they enable us to estimate more accurately the relevance and practical purpose of the theological doctrine of the Epistle. In particular, they provide a means by the aid of which it may be determined whether Hebrews was addressed to a Jewish-Christian audience, as tradition has ordinarily asserted, or to some other group, and what were the dangers to which the group was exposed.

The first of the passages in question occurs at the beginning of chapter ii. It comes in immediate sequence to the impressive prologue in which the writer, after declaring the finality of the Christian revelation, presents Jesus Christ, the Son, the Wisdom, and the Image of God, as enthroned at the right hand of the heavenly Majesty with a rank as much exceeding that of the angels as the name which He has inherited is superior to theirs. He then proceeds to admonition.

THE WORD OF JESUS AND THE WORD OF THE ANGELS (ii. 1-5)

Therefore we must give very special attention to the truths declared in our hearing, if we are not to drift from the course. If the word spoken by angels was valid, and all transgression and disobedience incurred its proper punishment, how shall we escape if we treat with unconcern a salvation so great as ours, one which, taking its beginning from the word spoken by the Lord, was certified to us by those who heard it, God bearing them out by the witness of signs and portents of various kinds, and by gifts of the Holy Spirit allotted in accordance with His will? For it is not to the angels that God has subjected the World to Come of which we speak.

The danger against which the readers are here asked very specially to guard is that of 'drifting' in the sense of slipping away from, or losing hold upon, the Christian salvation. A nautical metaphor is employed, but the meaning is further defined as neglecting or 'showing no concern about' the revelation of God in Christ. The passage does not explicitly name any competing object of attraction to which the community is falling away. No more is asserted than that there has been a slackening of interest in, a letting slip of the reality of the Christian message. The writer's next words, however, suggest that if what is denominated as *the word spoken by angels* was not itself the deflecting cause accounting for the aberration of these Christians, at any rate the reminder was needed that the Christian revelation was of more solemn import than that word. The writer, speaking of the Christian revelation, presents it under three aspects, which constitute its supreme claim to consideration: (1) There is its source in the word not of angels, but of Christ; (2) there is its attestation by men who had heard that word, and whose witness had been attended by every kind of numinous manifestation of power; (3) there is its eschatological character, or reference to the World to Come. 'It is not to the angels', says the writer very pointedly, 'that God has subjected the World to Come of which we speak.' Evidently the peril of the community was that of so lax a hold on the Christian realities as seriously to endanger its share in eternal salvation.

The antithesis in which *the word spoken through the Lord* is here set over against the word spoken through angels leaves the character of the issue in little doubt. The prominence given to Christ over the angels in the opening chapters of Hebrews has been explained sometimes by the hypothesis that the community addressed was tempted to angel-worship, a contingency not beyond the bounds of possibility in certain Jewish and even Christian circles,[1] or alternatively was in danger of falling away to syncretistic pagan religion, which, like the whole life of the pagan peoples, was believed in Judaism to stand under the government of the angels. Thus we find in Deuteronomy iv. 15 and 19-20 certain words of warning spoken to Israel which in the Septuagint version run: 'Take heed lest you lift up your eyes to heaven, and when you see the sun and the moon and the stars and all the universe (Heb. host) of heaven, you are led away and worship and serve them, things which the Lord your God has assigned to the (other) nations under heaven. But you the Lord has taken, and brought forth out of the iron furnace, out of Egypt, to be a special people of His own.' Again, in chapter

---

[1] Revelation of St. John xix. 10, xxii. 8.

D

xxxii. 8, we read in the same version the words: 'When the Most High apportioned the nations, when He scattered the sons of Adam, He fixed the bounds of the nations according to the number of the angels of God.'[1] Taking these two passages together, we see in Israel an association of the angels or 'host of heaven' with star-worship and other pagan practices, and indeed Rabbinical Judaism recognised angels of Rome, Egypt, Babylon, Media, Greece, and other countries, as well as of the elements, water, fire, wind, iron, and the like.[2] But neither to the one nor to the other of these errors, neither to angel-worship, though it raised its head at Colossae,[3] nor to astral religion and pagan practices in general, is there any allusion in the Epistle to the Hebrews. We seem, therefore, to be thrown upon another explanation which fortunately admits of easy recognition and certainly agrees better with the general character of the passage.

In Judaism the angels were the mediators and guardians of the *Law* of God. We have St. Paul's statement that 'the Law was ordained through angels by the hand of a mediator',[4] and, what is even more to the point here, we have Stephen's reminder to the unbelieving Jews that they had 'received the Law in charges from angels, and had not kept it'.[5] Assertions to the same effect occur in Josephus[6] and in the Rabbinical literature.[7] While it is not said expressly in our Hebrews passage that it was any fascination from the side of the Mosaic Law that was drawing the community away from the revelation of God in Jesus, the theory that

---

[1] See Strack-Billerbeck, Index under the word 'Engel'.
[2] *Ibid.*   [3] Colossians ii. 18, 23.   [4] Galatians iii. 19.
[5] Acts vii. 53.   [6] E.g. *Antiquities*, XV. 5. 3.
[7] Cf. Strack-Billerbeck, III. pp. 554-556, a rich storehouse of material.

some influence from this quarter was accountable for the deflection and relaxation of purpose with which the community is charged is not incompatible with the evidence of the section as a whole, and may be assumed provisionally as a reasonable explanation.

The final statement that it is not to the angels—who rule in this present world—that God has subordinated 'the World to Come' is significant as an indication of the writer's eschatology, his conviction that in Jesus eternity has made itself known in time, introducing a supreme crisis in religious history. Those, he means, who lose their grip on this gospel of the Ultimate Reality forfeit their share in the final salvation of God and in all that that salvation means. Judaism, indeed, as Dr. Moffatt points out, assigned to the angels in heaven a function of ministering and interceding to the Lord for the righteous, and making expiation for their sins of ignorance. The classical passage for this, in effect priestly, ministry or 'liturgy' of the archangels is Testament of Levi iii. 5-6, but Dr. R. H. Charles in his commentary on the Testaments cites also T. Dan. vi. 2: 'the angel that intercedeth for you . . . is a mediator between God and man'; T. Levi. v. 6: 'I am the angel who intercede for the nation of Israel'; 1 Enoch ix. 3: 'to you, the holy ones of heaven, the souls of men make their suit, saying, Bring our cause before the Most High', and other passages. A heavenly function is thus ascribed to the angels with reference to the supernal world. But for the writer to the Hebrews all such functions of these 'ministering spirits' have faded in the light of Christ as the stars pale when the sun has arisen. Christ alone is Lord of the World to Come.

The Heavenly Calling of Christians and the Eschatological Now (iii. 1-11)

The passage we have examined is followed at ii. 6 by a return of the writer to his expository theme. He turns from the exaltation of Christ above the angels to His supremacy with reference to man. Jesus is the Son of Man—though the writer to the Hebrews does not, any more than St. Paul, use that express title of Christ—who through the complete identification of Himself with humanity in life and in death was able to overthrow the devil's sovereignty in death, and has thus qualified Himself to become our High-Priest with God. The admonitory section which follows blends didactic matter with exhortation in a rather complicated fashion, but we may separate out certain strands of the argument as relevant to our practical purpose.

Therefore, holy brethren, you who share the heavenly calling, take note of Jesus, whom in our confession we acknowledge to be our Apostle and High-Priest. Jesus was faithful to the God who appointed Him, just as Moses was ' in all God's house'. Jesus has been accounted worthy of a higher glory than Moses (iii. 1-3).

Here (i) we find the writer concerned to stress the supernal character of the Christian course of life. The persons addressed are 'companions of the heavenly calling'. Heavenly calling is an expression which, like such other terms beloved of the writer as 'drawing near to God' or 'running the race set before us', reveals the characteristic orientation of his mind to the eschatological quality of the Christian life. It brings out the inevitable tension which is at the heart of that life. According to this writer, we have here no continuing

'city', nor even any present 'rest' in the life of the soul.
We are drawn by Jesus into a course which has its only
satisfaction and End in God. We shall be brought
back to this conception repeatedly.

(ii) In the same passage we find the writer emphasising again the transcendence of Jesus, but this time by
comparison not with the angels but with Moses. It is
possible that the citation of the Scriptural word that
Moses was 'faithful in all God's house'[1] reflects the
fact that the community at Rome in its situation of
Christian indecision was emphasising the dependable-
ness of the religion of the Law. The writer replies that
Jesus also is dependable, but Jesus as the Son of God
has received from God a higher standing and authority
than Moses.

Is it also possible—the point may be merely suggested
in passing—that in declaring Moses to be faithful, the
community at Rome was thinking that the religion of
the Law had at least its written books, a solid buttress
to which the new faith could not lay claim? Actually
there is no evidence in the Epistle of this being asserted.
The writer's appeal to the readers is that they consider
Jesus in Himself as the final revealer of God, whose
personal relation to God as 'Son' confers on Him an
authority transcending all other claims (i. 1-2). But in
Jewish-Christian circles of the first generation or two
the force of arguments based on the religion of the Book
may have created disquietude over against the religion
of the Spirit.

(iii) The writer presents Jesus as 'the Apostle and
High-Priest of our confession' (iii. 1). I have translated
these words in the form 'Jesus, whom we confess to

---

[1] Numbers xii. 7.

be our Apostle, etc.', giving *homologia* its normal and
natural sense.   There is no warrant or need for understanding the term here as an equivalent for 'religion'.
Christianity as known to the writer is the confession of
Jesus Christ as our High-Priest, and this for him is as
momentous as the confession 'Jesus is Lord' is for St.
Paul.[1]   It is true that Stephen did not, in so many
words, designate Jesus as our High-Priest, but the
conception is consonant enough with his reaction away
from the older cultus.   Nor is it likely that the primitive
Christian community, with the Messianic 110th Psalm
before it, was not familiar from the beginning with the
thought of Jesus as 'a priest for ever after the order of
Melchizedek'. [2]   Certainly the fact that in Hebrews
Jesus is presented to us as our High-Priest (ii. 17,
iii. 1, iv. 14-16), *before* there has been any theological
explanation or elaboration of the idea by the writer
(chapters vii.-x.), suggests that this office of Jesus
belongs to the *a priori* element, the charter-substance
of the received Christian faith.   And if the confession
also proclaims Jesus to be our 'Apostle', it should be
remembered that in Judaism the high-priest on the
Day of Atonement was recognised as the *Shaliach* (the
apostle, commissioner) not of men but of God.[3]

(iv) The writer insists on the critical importance of
the present moment in religious history.

We are His house if we keep our confidence and
exultant hope firm to the End.   Therefore the Holy
Spirit (specifies Today as the time.   He) says, 'Today,
if you hear His voice, do not harden your hearts as (your
fathers did) at the Provocation, on the day of the Tempta-

---

[1] Romans x. 8-9.   [2] Psalm cx. 4.
[3] Strack-Billerbeck, III. p. 4 cites *Qid.* 23*b* as authority.   See the
whole discussion of the term *Shaliach* on pp. 2-4.

tion in the desert. . . . So I swore in My anger, They shall never enter into My Rest ' (iii. 6-8, 11).

The author of Hebrews unquestionably regards his readers as placed in a situation of crisis comparable to that of Israel in the wilderness. The Christian life is, in fact, a new Exodus—not to an earthly place of rest, such as the old Israel was promised but failed to attain through unbelief, but to a heavenly Rest, an eternal kingdom of God. In such a journey everything depends on the maintenance, through 'confidence and exultant hope', of the original tension set up by the entrance into time of the call of God in Jesus. Jesus has announced the eternal order. Christians live in the ultimate period, the last 'Now' of time. The writer quotes Psalm xcv. 7-11 as the testimony of the Holy Spirit that the people of the Exodus missed the goal through not listening to God's voice. Hence their obstinacy, wandering, and final loss of their inheritance. They did not keep up by faith 'the march in God begun'. Now, says the writer, *God has declared again an ultimate chance, a final Now, a critical last Today of salvation*. Will the readers grasp again the supreme significance of the Eternal Moment inaugurated by Jesus and of the journey commenced in Him? While the appeal to the Exodus may not prove that Jewish-Christians are addressed, seeing that St. Paul in 1 Corinthians x. can similarly ground an appeal to a Gentile Church, there is nothing which makes against that assumption.

It can be argued that the author's reiterated emphasis on the 'forty years' of Israel's probation in the desert makes transparent the date of the Epistle to the Hebrews. Hebrews was written at a time when the fortieth anniversary of the dawning of salvation in Jesus (ii. 3) was

already at hand or at least in prospect, therefore in the
sixties of the first Christian century. This date agrees
so well with certain other features in the evidence for
Hebrews that the argument should not be dismissed,
as it is by Dr. Moffatt.[1]

It is in the light of the critical issues of the existing
situation that we must understand the appeals to the
readers which now follow.

Various Warnings relating to the Crisis
(iii. 12-iv. 13)

Look to it, brethren, lest there be in any of you a
wicked unbelieving heart tempting you to depart from
the living God (iii. 12).

We see that unbelief was the cause of their (Israel's)
not being able to enter in. While, then, the promise of
entrance into His Rest remains, let us be afraid of any
one of you being thought to have dropped behind (iii.
19-iv. 1).

We have become partners with Christ, if we keep our
initial confidence firm to the end, while the word 'Today' holds good (iii. 14 f.).

We have had the good news (of salvation) preached
to us, just as they had, but the message heard brought
no benefit to them, because they were not united in
faith with the (true, or believing) hearers (iv. 2).

Let us make it our aim, therefore, to enter into that
Rest (of God) that no man may fall through the same
sort of unbelief. For God's Word is alive and active
and cuts deeper than any two-edged sword. It penetrates to the separation of soul and spirit, joints and

[1] *Commentary*, p. 45.

marrow, and keenly discriminates between the thoughts and purposes of the mind (iv. 11-12).

On these passages only a few comments are necessary.

(*a*) The danger of the situation in the community appears everywhere as that of apostatising from the living God, and this through unbelief or infatuation wrought by sin. Nothing in the writer's language suggests a resurgence of pagan immorality, such as a Gentile-Christian community might be particularly exposed to, as the ground of this warning against sin. To the author, as to St. Paul,[1] everything which is not of *faith*, which in this case means every taking of the eyes off the Christian goal of life, every relaxation of the eschatological tension of the soul, would be sin. On the other hand, nothing in iii. 12, iii. 14-15, iii. 19-iv. 1 necessarily indicates a Jewish-Christian group as the recipients of the warning.

(*b*) In the passage about being 'partakers with Christ' (iii. 12-15) the author's conception of the norm of Christian life comes clearly to the front. There is in Hebrews nothing of the faith-mysticism of St. Paul which comes to expression in the doctrine of Christ 'in us' or us 'in Christ'. The eyes are outwardly and objectively directed towards Christ as the Pioneer, the Forerunner, and the Perfecter of our faith (xii. 1-2), and we are 'partakers with Christ' in the sense of being loyal to, and following Him into the life of the World to Come. Doubtless in this rapt engagement to keep Christ ever before our eyes there is involved so close and intimate a determination of our personal existence by Him that in a real, though not in the Pauline mystical sense, we may be said to be 'in Christ'. The

[1] Romans xiv. 23.

substance of the relationship implied may be the same in both cases, but the plastic form of the language used is different.

(c) Christianity means (iv. 11-12) a life in which we expose our whole existence at every point to the cutting edge, the trenchant judgment, the drastic operation of God's Word to us in Christ, a Word which as 'living' is incompatible with stagnation and death, and as 'active' gets things done. The life so laid open at every point to God's judgment upon us is the truly *eschatological* life, and has the nature of eternity already in it.

(d) Just as St. Paul reminds the Corinthians that the Old Testament people had the sacraments given to them at the Red Sea and in the desert, so the writer to the Hebrews reminds his group that the same people had the gospel of salvation preached to them, but the message brought no benefit to them, because

'They were not united in faith with those who heard it.'

If this is the right reading,[1] it admits of the inference being drawn that the Christian group at Rome whom the writer addresses was separating itself off in the matter of 'faith' from the true believing body of the Church. In terms of our hypothesis, a section of Jewish-Christian brethren was drawing apart from the mass of the Jewish and other Christians constituting the Church at Rome. There is, indeed, another reading, according to which the message did not benefit the old Israel 'because it (i.e. the word) was not united to faith on the part of those who heard it'. But the

[1] It is the reading of the mass of Uncial (BACD etc.) and other Greek MSS. The other reading is supported by א and a few Minuscules.

first reading, as the more difficult of the two, is to be preferred, and the acceptance of it in the sense above indicated advances very notably the understanding of our problem.

Summing up the results so far reached, we see that the community addressed in Hebrews, apparently under the influence of the Jewish Law or 'word spoken through the angels', was drifting from the truth of Christianity, and in danger of apostatising from the living God. It was revealing an unpardonable indifference to the momentous significance of Christian decision at a supreme moment in history. It was relaxing its hold on Christ in whom the Eternal World had announced itself. It was not exposing itself to the judgment of God's living Word, and one result was that it was withdrawing, or tending to withdraw itself, from the Church's larger fellowship of faith.

NECESSITY OF ADVANCING FROM FIRST PRINCIPLES TO THE FULL KNOWLEDGE OF THE CHRISTIAN MYSTERY (v. 11-vi. 18)

In chapter v. 1-10 the writer turns to the divine character and institution of the office of Christ as our High-Priest, quoting Psalm cx. 4, and describing in moving terms how Jesus in 'the days of His flesh' was 'perfected' by His prayers and intercessions to God, His passionate crying and tears, and His godly obedience learned through suffering. So He was qualified to become our High-Priest with God and 'the author of an eternal salvation'. Speaking with reference to the mystery of this Priesthood, the writer confesses the difficulty of finding words by which he can explain himself to his readers.

About this I have much to say, and it is difficult to explicate the meaning since you have become dull of hearing. At a time when you ought by experience to be teaching others, you are in need of some one instructing you over again in the very rudiments of divine revelation (v. 11-12).

The writer's difficulty is that his hearers are backward hearers who have remained virtually at the A B C stage of religious understanding. The sally that they need elementary instruction at a time when they ought to be teaching others excludes the possibility of the community in question being regarded as an intellectual *élite* of some kind to whom the writer desires to communicate some higher Christian *gnosis*. The latter view is, indeed, defended by Dr. E. F. Scott,[1] who thinks that the very abstruseness which the writer feels to be inseparable from his argument at this point is itself essential to the hortatory purpose in the writer's mind. An effort of thought is required in order to lead the community out of its complacent contentment with the mere elementary principles of faith.

It is difficult, however, not to think that this interpretation exaggerates the intellectual side of the author's appeal. All that is necessarily implied is that it is time that these backward Christians at Rome came to a mature understanding of the kind of *life* to which from the beginning they were as Christians committed. Something is retarding the advance from first principles which might have been expected of them.

Let us therefore leave behind us the elementary principles of Christian teaching, and bear forwards to a

[1] *The Epistle to the Hebrews*, pp. 30 f., 42-45, 194 f. Cf. Dr. A. Nairne, *The Epistle of Priesthood*, pp. 22 f.

realisation of results. We cannot always be laying foundations in terms of repentance from dead works, faith in God, instruction about baptisms and imposition of hands, the resurrection of the dead and eternal judgment (vi. 1-2).

What the writer proposes is not necessarily to advance into new realms of truth or to develop a *gnosis* of the Christian religion. His purpose may be merely to lead his hearers from superficial apprehensions of the life to which they are as Christians committed, by asking for a follow-up in appropriate action. Are they going forward from the first principles of their confession, or are they going back upon these principles? In the latter case the foundations would need to be laid all over again, and this the writer deprecates. Nothing, however, really justifies us in saying that he is indifferent or superior to Christian 'beginnings'. That has been asserted, and a contrast has been drawn in this respect between him and St. Paul, who does not treat the fundamental verities of the faith as a stage that may be left behind.[1] As against this criticism, it is only necessary to compare certain words of the latter in his Epistle to the Philippians, which speak of whole reaches of Christian apprehension and attainment not yet achieved by him towards which nevertheless he presses. The admission that these further stages of cognition and achievement exist does not, however, imply that the Christian knowledge in question needs to be developed *speculatively* in a Gnostic direction, and no more need we read that idea into the mind of the writer to the Hebrews. St. Paul's meaning is unambiguous, and both in form and substance it affords a very

[1] So E. F. Scott, *The Epistle to the Hebrews*, p. 76.

excellent parallel to our author's plea. 'My one purpose is, forgetting the things behind me, and reaching out to those before me, to press to the goal for the prize of God's high calling in Christ Jesus. Let all of us who are mature share this purpose with me.' [1] At this point St. Paul is as much an eschatologist as is our author.

It is a tenable view, therefore, that the persons addressed in Hebrews were immature Christians needing more of the gospel, rather than immature theologians whom the author wished to initiate into a higher *gnosis*.

As for the foundations which the teacher cannot always be re-laying—repentance from dead works, faith in God, instruction about baptisms, etc.—there is no ground for inferring that the persons appealed to were of Gentile extraction, since Jews would not have needed indoctrination on such points. Even Jewish Christians might be backward Christians. Moreover, Jesus had to speak to Jews about repentance from dead works,[2] and about faith in God.[3] He had to speak to His 'Hebrew' Church about the difference of John's baptism from His own.[4] A Hellenist-Jewish convert, Apollos, had also to be initiated into the distinction between the two rites,[5] and the experience of the Ephesian group in Acts xix. suggests the significance for—presumably Jewish—converts of the 'imposition of hands' in sequence to baptism. As for the 'resurrection of the dead' and 'eternal judgment', Jewish converts, even more than others, needed to learn the new meaning which these ideas had acquired through the Christian

---

[1] Philippians iii. 12 f.   [2] Cf. Matthew v. 20.
[3] Cf. Mark xi. 23 f.; Luke xviii. 8.
[4] Acts i. 5.   [5] Acts xviii. 24-26.

revelation. The passage, therefore, is perfectly compatible with the Jewish extraction of the group addressed, and may even be held to favour it.

For it is an impossible thing for the once enlightened, who have tasted the heavenly gift, who have become participants in the Holy Spirit, who have tasted the good word of God and the powers of the Age to Come, and fall away—it is an impossible thing to bring them to a new repentance, since they crucify the Son of God for themselves, and expose Him to contempt (vi. 4-6).

This is one of the most famous and, historically, one of the most debated passages in the Epistle to the Hebrews. In the point of its denial of a 'second repentance' Tertullian defended Hebrews as against the laxer doctrine of the Pastor of Hermas, which allowed defaulters a second chance. Tertullian's judgment is definite enough. Accepting Hebrews as a work of Barnabas,[1] he writes:

'Et utique receptior apud ecclesias epistola Barnabae illo apocrypho Pastore moechorum.'

Montanists and Novatians also appealed to the Epistle to the Hebrews at this point.

The interest of the passage for us is the light which it throws on the historical situation of the readers. The writer is not giving expression to general truths, but assumes, for the sake of argument, that the falling away in question is an accomplished fact. The Christians addressed, after receiving through Christ the blessings and gifts of the New Age—note the terms 'heavenly gift', 'Holy Spirit', 'powers of the Age to Come'—fall away. They take thereby an irreversible step. In

---

[1] See above, pp. 10 f.

the heavenly gift, in the Holy Spirit, and in the powers of the Age to Come, Ultimate Reality has projected itself into time through Christ. It has laid hold on these Christians not simply as enlightenment or truth, but as life and power. If as Christians they fall away from it, what then? It has been imagined that the reference is to a relapse to Judaism, actual or prospective, on the part of the group. Through disappointment with Christianity because of persecution and the delay of the Lord's coming, this group is thinking to recover religious integrity by reverting to the older faith. On this view the second repentance which is declared 'an impossible thing' is re-integration into Judaism.[1] But this is not in itself a natural interpretation of the passage. As the writer does not say to what the group is resiling, nothing more can be inferred than that it is falling away from Christ. On the other hand, the further statement that such persons are 'crucifying' Christ for themselves is at least patient of the interpretation that they are *virtually* putting themselves in the position of the Jews.

But, though I speak like this, beloved, I am persuaded in your case of better things, things that connect with salvation. God is not unjust: He does not forget your work and the love you have shown for His sake in the service which you have rendered and are rendering now to the saints. But I long that each one of you should show an equal zeal to attain full assurance in your hope right to the end, so that, instead of being inert, you should live up to the example of those who inherit the promises by their faith and patience (vi. 9-12).

It would appear, then, that the catastrophe predicted in the last section was hypothetical rather than real.

[1] Above, p. 14, and Nairne, *The Epistle of Priesthood*, pp. 13 ff.

The community's work and love, shown for God's sake in still continued service to the Church as a whole, is a sign that they have not dropped out of the purpose of God. But the writer would fain see in all of its members a greater tensity of forward-looking and expectant faith. He sees them listless, uncertain, not keyed to the standard of those who by faith and patience attain the promised inheritance of God.

THE CONSECRATED WAY.—THE CALL TO FAITH AND HOLINESS (vi. 19-20; x. 19-31)

The Christian inheritance is in eternity, not in any present possession or experience of the soul. Christians are 'refugees of God' (vi. 18), persons who have sought asylum, ultimate deliverance as offered in Him. And between us and the fruition of the eschatological hope a link exists—Jesus, our Forerunner, our High-Priest.

This hope we hold to as to an anchor of the soul, unslipping and unyielding, and reaching into the world within the Veil. There Jesus has entered in advance of us, having become High-Priest for ever after the order of Melchizedek (vi. 19-20).

In terms of this fine metaphor Jesus is the Forerunner (*prodromos*), who has passed on into the heavenly world, carrying with Him the anchor to which our souls are made firm. We may connect this conception of the Forerunner with what was said earlier of the specific character of Stephen's futurist outlook: we do not wait passively for the Lord to come to us from heaven, but we go out, so to speak, towards Him and the heavenly world.[1]

[1] See above, pp. 32 f.

E

In chapters vii.-ix., which here intervene, the writer develops his didactic theme—the Priesthood and the Sacrifice of Christ—making use for this purpose of the Alexandrian conception of the Two Worlds with its contraposition of heavenly reality and earthly shadow. In chapter x. he comes to grips again with the historical situation of his readers.

My brothers, now that we have confidence to enter God's holy place through the blood of Jesus, by the new, living way which He has instituted for us through the Veil (which means His flesh), and have a great High-Priest over the house of God, let us draw near with a sincere heart, in full assurance of faith, having our hearts sprinkled from an evil conscience and our bodies washed in pure water. Let us hold, without any deviation, to the hope which we confess to be ours, for He who has promised can be trusted: and let us study how to stimulate one another to love and good works (x. 19-24).

We find here again the familiar notes to which our ears have become accustomed in the practical teaching of the Epistle—'confidence', 'full assurance of faith', 'undeviating hope'. These are qualities in which the writer knows the community to be weakening through the taking of their eyes off the transcendent heavenly end of their vocation. But something more is added here, as we should expect, now that the writer in chapters vii.-ix. has brought to full expression his thought of 'the one true, pure, immortal sacrifice' which our great High-Priest has made for us.

In this passage we have perhaps the supreme expression of the writer's thought of the Christian life as worshipful approach through Christ to God. In St. Paul's letters the note of worship is constantly present, as for example where he says that Abraham believed, 'giving glory to God'[1]; St. Paul, no more than the writer to the Hebrews, can think of a faith which has not adoration at the heart of it. But in Hebrews the whole pattern of Christian life is conceived in terms of worship. That life is a continuous, and indeed eternal approach to the holy Presence of God. But it is to the heavenly, not to the earthly Holy of Holies that we now draw near, and we enter not by way of the ancient sacrifices for the removal of our guilt, but 'through the blood of Jesus'. We go by the new, living way which Christ has instituted, and we go as the cleansed, as those who have 'our hearts purified by sprinkling from an evil conscience' as well as 'our bodies washed in pure water'. We have an unmistakable reference here to Christian baptism as the rite which from the first days of the Church signified destination for, and proleptic entrance into the eternal Kingdom of God, the sphere of salvation. So our life is conceived as an ever-deepening entrance into the mystery of fellowship with God. It is an ever-increasing response to the Manifestation of God, and if the writer describes the way as a 'living' way, it is because it is not by the lifeless works or dead victims of the old religion that we are prepared and purified for access to God, but by the living Christ who has entered the heavenly Sanctuary in advance of us, pleading His atonement.

The writer speaks of this way as 'through the Veil'. The metaphor is derived from the curtain in the Tabernacle which hung between the outer sanctuary and the Holy of Holies (ix. 2-9). Here by a mystical-allegorical touch the writer identifies the Veil with the 'flesh' of Christ. The Gospels speak of the veil of the

[1] Romans iv. 20.

Temple, the barrier which hung between God and man, as rent at the death of Christ. The writer to the Hebrews, as Dr. Moffatt trenchantly puts it, 'allegorises the veil as the flesh of Christ; this had to be rent before the blood could be shed, which enabled Him to enter and open God's presence for the people'.[1]

But that this conception of Christian life as Approach, Worship, the supra-ritual Purification and Sanctification of our spirits, signifies no indifference to the practical task of holy living is made clear by the exhortation not only to faith, but to sincerity, love, and good works. Our author's concentration on worship as the essential form of the religious life is not, therefore, justly represented when it is said that there is not in Hebrews, as in St. Paul, a passing from ritual ideas to an inward 'reasonable service'. In Hebrews worship is the norm of life, but it is a worship which is sublimated, though not subjectivised. In its out-going activity and its continuous upward direction of the soul towards God and the heavenly world the whole regeneration of our spiritual and moral nature is subsumed and included.

Let us not discontinue meeting together, as the habit of some is. Rather let us exhort each other, the more so that you see the Day drawing near (x. 25).

This injunction follows appropriately on the reminder about love and good works in the previous section. But what is this desertion of the common 'meeting' of which the community is here accused, allusively rather than directly, in the reference to 'some' whose custom this is? (1) We know that Christians with Gnostic leanings were in the habit sometimes of seceding from the

---

[1] *Commentary*, p. 143.

Church.[1] And the same might hold true of conservative
Jewish Christians not in full sympathy with the freedom
from legal and ceremonial observances practised by the
larger Church. On this interpretation—see what has
been said above on iv. 2—the gathering which is being
forsaken is that of the Church as a whole.[2] The defaulters are a minority group. But there is (2) another
possible interpretation which I would suggest as
deserving of consideration. The gathering which is
being forsaken is the private gathering which the
minority itself has been accustomed to observe, but
which is now falling into desuetude through the weakening of the impulse of Christian faith within the group.

On this hypothesis it would be open to us to suppose
that a group of Jewish Christians derived from, or
possibly still continuing to exist within, a Jewish synagogue at Rome was under stress of one kind or another
—opposition, persecution, disappointment—giving up
its Christian meetings and virtually dissolving back
into the general life of the Jewish community. On the
same hypothesis the word *episynagoge*, which is here
used, might be given the sense of 'epi-synagogue', or
Christian appendage to the Jewish synagogue. Elsewhere, however, the word simply means gathering, and
while the dissolution of a Jewish-Christian group into
the general life of Judaism would not, under certain
circumstances, be incredible, nothing in the writer's
language justifies us in carrying our hypothesis to this
extreme. It is not even definitely indicated in the
passage that the group was Jewish-Christian, though
the probability that it was is a strong one.

For if we sin deliberately, after we have attained to

[1] Cf. 1 John ii. 18 f.   [2] Above, pp. 58 f.

the knowledge of the truth, there remains no sacrifice (which can be offered) for sins, but only a dreadful expectation of judgment, and fiery wrath destined to consume the enemies (of God) (x. 26-27).

With this passage we should compare the section vi. 4-6 discussed above.[1] The sin referred to is quite definitely rejection of the truth, contempt for the revelation of God in Christ. The writer speaks of the death-penalty attaching to defiance of the law of Moses, and he then adds:

How much greater a punishment will the man be judged to have incurred, who has trampled on the Son of God, profaned the blood of the covenant by which he was sanctified, and outraged the Spirit of grace! . . . It is a terrible thing to fall into the hands of the living God (x. 29-30).

The nature of the sin warned against is stated in its fearful reality, and the language—'trampling on the Son of God', etc.—has a terrible gravity. Of whom is the writer thinking? In an earlier comment on the language of the parallel section vi. 4-6 it was observed that the words 'they crucify the Son of God for themselves' were patient of the interpretation that the persons in question were Christians who were putting themselves in the position of the Jews. Here the language has a more general character and does not absolutely decide whether this flagrant rejection of the Christian revelation, this trampling on the Son of God, is by a Jewish-Christian group resiling backwards from, or by another group 'going forward' beyond Christ, as Gnostically-minded brethren tended to do.[2]

---

[1] Above, pp. 63 f.   [2] Cf. again 1 John ii. 18 f.

A REMINISCENCE AND AN ASSURANCE.—THE ADVENT OF CHRIST (x. 32-39)

Recall, however, the former days, after your enlightenment, when you stood up to a hard ordeal of suffering, being now publicly exposed in your own persons to insults and hardships, and now associated with others who were so treated. For you had sympathy with the imprisoned, and cheerfully accepted the seizure of your goods, knowing that yourselves had a better, an enduring inheritance. Do not now fling away that courage, which has in it the promise of a great reward. Patience is necessary that you may do the will of God and get fulfilment of the promise. For in ever so short a time now the Coming One will arrive, He will linger no more. And 'My righteous one shall live by his faith: if he resiles, My soul has no pleasure in him'. But we are not for resiling and being lost, but for believing and winning the soul (x. 32-39).

A deeply interesting historical reference to the early fortunes of the group addressed. If we suppose—and there is no reason to reject the assumption—that the ordeal referred to in the passage points back to the disturbances created at Rome by the edict of the Emperor Claudius in A.D. 49,[1] the persons addressed will have belonged to the original nucleus, the charter-members, so to speak, of the Church at Rome, and will, therefore, in all probability have been of Jewish extraction. This presumption cannot, of course, be proved, nor can any decisive conclusion be drawn from the action of 'resiling' or drawing back which the writer imputes to the group in its present trend. We cannot venture to say, on the strength of the language alone,

[1] See above, pp. 40 f.

that the lapse in question was in the Jewish direction and not, say, to sheer irreligion.

On the other hand, there is one part of the section from which more positive inferences may reasonably be drawn. This is the assurance given in verse 37:

'In ever so short a time now the Coming One will arrive, He will linger no more.'

More clearly than anywhere else in the Epistle, it would appear that disappointment over the delay of the Parousia of Christ was one cause at least of the community's apathy and loss of faith. Such disappointment might, of course, be general, affecting all types of Christians in the Church. In view, however, of the character of the primitive Christian outlook before the time of Stephen, it is at least legitimate to ask whether it would not be felt by Jewish Christians within the Church more sharply and characteristically than by others. While Stephen and the greater part of the world-mission Church, at Rome as elsewhere, believed that the Church must anticipate the return of Christ by going out into the world and preaching the gospel to all the nations,[1] the early 'Hebrew' community at Jerusalem looked for Christ to come to them, restoring the Kingdom to 'Israel'. If the group at Rome leaned in this latter direction, the re-assurance given them by the writer would have special point and relevance.

All we can say for certain, however, is that the group was losing its hold on the glory and hope of its eschato-

---

[1] Cf. the evidence of the Synoptic Gospels on the point. In the Parousia discourse in Mark xiii. 10 we read: 'to all the nations must the gospel first be preached.' In Matthew xxiv. 14 this takes the expanded form: 'this gospel of the Kingdom will be preached in all the world, for a witness to the nations; and then will the End come.'

logical calling, which demanded a perseverance in faith allowing of no relaxation of the original tension set up in the soul. Nevertheless, the writer ends on the note of hope. He expresses his confidence that his readers will reconsider the position. Including them with himself and the larger Church, he says: 'We are not for resiling and being lost, but for believing and winning the soul.'

THE NATURE AND FUNCTION OF FAITH
(xi. 1-40)

The great chapter on Faith follows appropriately on the words about not resiling and being lost but believing and winning the soul. The supra-historical character of the religious life is stressed, illustrations of its transcendent quality being drawn from the heroic figures of the Old Testament history from Abel to the Maccabean martyrs. The chapter is in this respect a reaffirmation and expansion of Stephen's great review of the same history in Acts vii.,[1] but there are some significant differences of emphasis. The writer is addressing his oration, not like Stephen to the Jews, but to a group of Christian people. There is, therefore, nothing in his statement of that indictment of the Jews for their apostasy and rejection of the prophets and messengers of God which is so marked a feature of Stephen's pronouncement; the rebellion, for example, of the Exodus generation against Moses [2] is not even mentioned. On the other hand, there is an even stronger accenting of that trumpet-call to 'Go out', which Stephen's ear detected everywhere in the Old Testament record, and

---

[1] See above, Chapter II, pp. 30-36.   [2] Acts vii. 35-40.

which for him was the keynote of God's whole calling of His people Israel.

For the purposes of our present study we are concerned mainly with the practical and admonitory bearings of the writer's exposition. It falls into three easily recognisable sections. In the first (xi. 1-6) a definition of faith is given in terms of its primary character as subjective apprehension of the reality of the invisible world. The second section (xi. 7-16) passes on to the essentially eschatological bearing of this reality upon present life and action. In the third section (xi. 17-40) the writer dwells on the trials, endurances, heroisms, sacrifices, privations and martyrdoms, as well as triumphs, which have been the concomitants and consequences of faith throughout the history of revealed religion. In the illustrative record the figures which stand out most prominently are Abraham, Moses, and the heroes and martyrs of the later period.

1. The writer begins with a definition of faith.

Faith is a firm assurance with regard to the objects of our hope. It is a conviction of the reality of the invisible world. It was for this quality that the men of old had witness borne to them. By faith we conceive the worlds to have been fashioned by the word of God, the visible order taking its origin out of invisible things (xi. 1-3).

The word *hypostasis* which is here rendered 'firm assurance' means literally a 'standing or existing under', and is used variously in Greek writers to express the ideas of support, basis, substructure or substratum, underlying reality, strength or firmness, character, purpose, substance and the like. As applied to the temporal process, it can signify duration, the basic principle underlying time, and so it occurs in one or two notable passages in the Septuagint version of the Psalms.[1] As applied to things, it connotes origin, foundation, structure, substance. As applied to mental and moral qualities and states, it indicates steadiness, firmness, assurance, persuadedness and the like.

The two principal senses between which we have to choose in the present passage are (i) substance, reality, essence, and (ii) confidence, firmness of persuasion, certitude. In the first of these two senses *hypostasis* is employed in Hebrews i. 3 to express that essence or being of God of which Christ is the reflex or stamp. But this sense is not admissible in the present context, for it cannot by any stretch of imagination be supposed that the writer understands faith to confer reality on things which have no substance or existence in themselves.[2] What faith does is to recognise what are here called 'invisible' things as the supreme realities and to make them determinative of the life of religion. We must adopt, therefore, the second of the above senses of the word, and understand *hypostasis* here to signify a mental condition of assurance regarding, or confidence in, the objects of religious hope. This is the meaning in chapter iii. 14 where the participation of Christians with Christ is made conditional upon the keeping of their initial assurance firm to the end.[3] So in the present passage faith is that subjective apprehension of transcendent realities by which these realities become basic and all-determinative for the religious life. Similarly the term *elenchos*, rendered

---

[1] Cf. Psalm xxxviii. 6 (LXX) : 'My duration of age is as nothing before Thee ' ; Psalm lxxxviii. 48 (LXX) : ' Remember how brief is my duration of life.'

[2] As Greek patristic exegetes like John Chrysostom thought. See Moffatt's note.

[3] Cf. the similar use of the word in 2 Corinthians ix. 4, xi. 17.

'conviction' in the above translation, primarily denotes test or proof, but here through the exigencies of the writer's argument it is given an extension of range by which it includes the inward principle of persuadedness or certitude which answers to the objective evidence offered. The life of faith is by both terms grounded on cognitive assent to the reality of heavenly things, but this assent by the very nature of its objects carries with it the acceptance of a transcendent value and use for life. From being a cognitive act faith passes into a principle regulating and inspiring behaviour. Its motives are existential.

What this signifies for the group of Christians addressed by the writer of Hebrews will be presently made apparent. Meantime he points out that such faith has been the distinguishing mark of all true religion since the world began (xi. 2); it underlies the Biblical doctrine of divine creation, according to which the understanding and the use of all life depend on the absoluteness of God's Word (xi. 3); faith also won for Abel the enduring title of 'the righteous' because it conformed his religion to the character of God, and for Enoch it procured the testimony that he 'pleased' God. What is revealed in such types of faith is not only belief in God's existence, but ardent commitment of life to God's justice, grace, and award (xi. 4-6).

2. The writer now shows from the record of the past how faith as apprehension and appropriation of the reality of the invisible world involves a choice between that world and the present order of things. He instances, in particular, Noah and Abraham.

By faith Noah, when warned by God of events not yet in sight, reverently prepared an ark for the salvation of his household: and by this act he condemned the world, and became an inheritor of the righteousness that accords with faith (xi. 7).

The nature of the decision required by faith, the 'Either-or' with which it confronts us, comes clearly here to the light. Noah's act involved the recognition that the present world was, in God's sight, in the wrong, but he did not on that account hesitate to make his choice. And so he entered into possession of that state of 'rightness with God' which answers to, or follows upon faith. Without such decision of faith this inheritance would not, in the sinful state of the world, have been reached. An even clearer case was Abraham's.

By faith Abraham, when called, obeyed by going out to a place which he was to receive as an inheritance; he went out without any knowledge of where he was going. By faith he became a temporary settler in a land which, though promised to him, was to him like a foreign country. He housed in tents with Isaac and Jacob, his co-inheritors in the same promise, for he looked for the City which was solidly founded, whose builder and maker was God (xi. 8-10).

Hebrews and Stephen (Acts vii. 2-7) alike start from Genesis xii. for their exposition of Abraham's faith, not like St. Paul from Genesis xv. 6. Abraham's faith was shown by his act of abandoning home and country for an invisible inheritance in the future, and by his acceptance of the lot of a landless *ger* in the present world. He was a displaced person, who wandered with his descendants in an alien environment until he died, and his frail tent-home never ceased to contrast with the city of God's foundation on which at the divine call he had staked his all. Sarah's faith also is commemorated as an illustration (xi. 11-12).

All these died believing. The promises did not come home to them here. They only saw and hailed them at a distance, and acknowledged that they were foreigners and sojourners on earth. Yes, people who speak like this make it plain that they are in quest of a country of their own. If their thought went back to the land out of which they came, they would have opportunity to revert to it. As it is, they long for a better, that is to say, a heavenly country, and therefore God is not ashamed to be named by them their God. He has indeed prepared a city for them (xi. 13-16).

The relevance of these moving words to the situation of a backward-looking, disappointed, ostracised group of Christians in the world's capital city needs no exposition.

3. The writer passes lastly to the triumphs wrought by faith in Biblical history, and to the tests, endurances, sacrifices, and heroisms which have been inseparable from its transcendent decisions. Abraham's readiness to sacrifice Isaac is instanced; it was an act which illustrated and anticipated the Christian faith in the Resurrection (xi. 17-19). The tenacity of Isaac, Jacob, and Joseph in holding to the divine promise of 'the things to come' is next mentioned (xi. 20-22). But the supreme example is the faith of Moses, whose choice and sacrifice made possible, under God, the Exodus of the people of God from Egypt and the Covenant made with that people at Sinai (xi. 23-29).

By faith Moses, when grown to manhood, declined to be called the son of Pharaoh's daughter, preferring to share ill-usage with the people of God than to spend a transient life in the indulgence of sin. He deemed the reproach of Christ a richer wealth than Egypt's treasures, for his eye was to the divine reward. By faith he left Egypt, not from fear of the king's anger: he was as one who saw the (King) invisible, and so held out. By faith he observed the Passover and the rite of the Blood-aspersion, that the Destroyer might not touch their first-born (xi. 24-28).

The points here emphasised in illustration of the character and consequences of Moses' act of faith— his vision of the Invisible One, his refusal to continue under the shelter and privilege of the Egyptian court, his choice of suffering with the people of God, his definite decision thereby to accept 'the reproach of Christ' in preference to the richest treasure on earth, his steady eye to the ultimate reward—would scarcely be missed by the Christians to whom the author of Hebrews was writing. They too have been called to a life of renunciation with the people of God. They too— on the hypothesis of their Jewish extraction—have had to give up an earlier position of imperial privilege under the *religio licita* of Judaism. They too must face the reproach incurred by their belief in Jesus as the Messiah, and must endure obloquy and material impoverishment for the sake of an eschatological award. They will see now that Moses himself, the institutor of the Passover rite and the cultus, was a confessor of Christ by the nature of his supreme choice and a participator in His sorrows, and is thus to be reckoned as one with the Christian people of God. When the writer says that Moses chose 'the reproach of Christ', the words admit of being understood in a purely analogical sense: Moses by throwing in his lot with the oppressed Hebrews was indeed accepting the same kind of contumely to which Jesus afterwards was subjected. But it is more in accordance with the writer's general understanding of the Old Testament history to consider that what he means here is that the Christ, the pre-incarnate Son of God, was actually a participant in the events of the Exodus, and Moses, when he made his great decision, *ipso facto* accepted and identified himself with the Christ's sufferings. In this way, though the point is not explicitly made, the Passover and the Blood-sprinkling which Moses instituted in Judaism are to be integrated with, and finally fulfilled in the redemption wrought by Jesus.

The accentuation in the passage of the 'reproach of Christ' hints that the supreme difficulty which the circle of Christians appealed to in the Epistle had to face was the misrepresentation and disparagement to which their confession of Jesus as the Christ exposed them, and which perhaps they contrasted painfully with tne privilege and security enjoyed by Judaism under the Roman imperial administration. Over against this the writer exalts the splendid and indeed stupendous achievements of the hero-judges, princes, and prophets of Israel from the age of the Exodus onwards, and the renunciations which were made for the sake of righteousness down to, and including the Maccabean martyrs for the Law (xi. 29-38). The writer does not touch on the redemptive value of these martyrdoms as the Maccabean literature does,[1] but he dwells on the faith which, casting away the hope of deliverance here, laid hold on the assurance of 'a better resurrection' hereafter.

These all established a name for faith, but the Promise

---

[1] Cf. IV Maccabees vi. 28 f., xvii. 21 f.

did not come home to them (here). God had something better in view for us, (and so purposed) that they should not attain the Perfection apart from us (xi. 39-40).

As Dr. Moffatt interprets it, 'God in His good providence reserved the Messianic *teleiosis* of Jesus Christ, until we could share it'.[1] In other words, the Christian people of God are to be integrated with the heroes and martyrs of the past in the felicity of the last, heavenly consolation. What this requires of the Christians addressed in the Epistle is stated in chapter xii.

THE CLOUD OF WITNESSES
(xii. 1-3)

Therefore, as we have so vast a throng of witnesses surrounding us, let us discard every encumbrance and besetting sin, and run with steady purpose the course appointed for us, directing our eyes towards Jesus, the Pioneer and the Consummator of faith. He for the sake of the joy appointed for Him bravely accepted the Cross, disregarding its shame, and He has taken His seat at the right hand of God. Just reflect what it meant for Him to face so courageously all that opposition of sinful men to Himself—that you may not grow faint and weary in your souls (xii. 1-3).

This summons follows appropriately on the great exposition of Faith, and the citation of heroic examples from the past history of religion in chapter xi. The passage gives supreme and classical expression to the writer's outlook on the Christian life, emphasising the upward objective direction of its vision, and the eschatological nature of its goal. In his comments on Hebrews xi. Dr. E. F. Scott remarks that, in one respect, the

[1] *Commentary*, p. 191.

F

idea of faith here expounded is 'not fully Christian',
for it finds its inspiration and typology in lives untouched by definite Christian influences.[1]   It may be
replied that this is to overlook the two considerations,
(1) that for the author the eschatological calling of
God has had one and the same character in all the ages,
both when, as in the Old Testament past, salvation was
descried only as a promise, and when, as now, it has
entered through Jesus on its fulfilment-phase; (2) that
for the author Christ was already present in the Old
Testament history,[2] so that the response of the heroes
of faith to the calling of God was in a real sense a
response to Him.   That at any rate would seem to be
the implication of the present passage.

The 'cloud' of witnesses now seen to be surrounding
the Christian community on earth may suggest to us
the mental picture of the packed throng of spectators
in an amphitheatre which shimmers or swims before
the eyes of the agonists in the arena.   But in reality
it is not towards us that these witnesses have their faces
turned but towards Jesus, whom they already truly
beheld when they endured 'as seeing Him who is
invisible'; and it is not because their eyes are upon us
that we are to throw off every encumbrance and the
sin which so easily gets round us, but because we are
engaged in the same conflict or contest as the 'witnesses'
were, and must look for inspiration in the same direction.
Athletes in the lists of faith, Christians are to divest
themselves of all that hampers or betrays them into
sin.   In the case of those Christians whom the writer
has in mind the allusion may well be to the retarding
or seductive influence of memories or sentiments which

---

[1] *The Epistle to the Hebrews*, pp. 190 f.
[2] See above, pp. 79 f., and below, pp. 96, 144, 184-187.

date from their Jewish past, before the time when the fulfilment-phase of God's calling announced itself in Jesus. In any case it is not to the past or to the environing world or even into their own souls that Christians are to look, but towards Jesus who, as He has started His people on the eternal course of life, will see them to the finish. The writer cites the supreme example given us in Jesus' own acceptance of the Cross despite the 'shame' which it involved. It is in His spirit that we must face the obloquy and suffering which our confession of faith in Him involves. Here two brief comments fall to be made.

First, the words above translated 'for the sake of the joy appointed for Him' admit also of being rendered 'in exchange for (or in place of) the joy appointed for Him', and they are so understood by some expositors. The reference will then be to the pre-incarnate bliss which the Son of God renounced in order to accept and fulfil His redeeming office. But though that conception finds expression in St. Paul, especially in the great passage Philippians ii. 5 ff., the writer to the Hebrews never speaks of the Redeemer's sacrifice in terms of a pre-incarnate renunciation, and therefore the ordinary understanding of the words ought to be preferred.

Secondly, the writer relates the sacrifice of Christ to His courageous facing of 'so great an opposition of sinners to Himself'. This is the great 'analogy' of faith on which the Christians addressed are to meditate in case they should grow faint and weary in their souls. The Cross of Jesus takes its character from His supreme act of faith in accepting and enduring all that 'fearful enmity of the carnal heart of man towards God' which raged around Him on Calvary; and redemption, the consummation of the course of the faithful life, demands of Christians the same kind of courage when confronted by similar contradiction. But there is a variant reading which for 'the opposition of sinners to Himself' has 'the opposition of sinners to themselves', which would suggest, as the most appalling feature of the apocalypse of evil which broke out against Jesus, the riot of self-contradiction going on in men's own hearts. We might then think of the mutually refutative charges brought against Him by false witnesses at His trial before the Sanhedrin or while He hung on the Cross. But while the English Revised Version and numerous scholars prefer this as the more difficult of the two readings, it is not at all certain that either of the two readings, 'against Himself' or 'against themselves', stood in the original text. They may have originated as alternative glosses noted in the margin of an archetype which did not specify against whom the 'contradiction' was directed. So Dr. Moffatt in his *Commentary* on the passage.[1]

OTHER EXHORTATIONS

(xii. 5-17, xiii. 1-8, 15-25)

The writer follows up his main appeal by the addition of various concluding admonitions, the first of them an exhortation to submit to that 'discipline' which Christians must expect as 'sons' of God (xii. 5-11). He then reverts to the self-discipline which regard for the final object of the Christian journey demands as

---

[1] ' Against himself ' is the reading of A P, some codices of the Latin Vulgate, the Harkleian Syriac, and the mass of Greek MSS. ' Against themselves ' is read by ℵ D and the Latin and Syriac Vulgates.

against slack hands, weak knees, and lameness (xii.
12-13). The injunction to seek 'peace with all men',
as necessary to that 'consecration' without which no
one shall attain to the eschatological vision of God,
may be an indirect rebuke to the separatist tendencies
of a reactionary minority; 'missing the grace of God'
and allowing a 'root of bitterness' to spring up with
troublesome and demoralising consequences for the
community may refer—as the echo of the language of
Deuteronomy xxix. 18 shows—to the religious infidelity
into which the minority's lapse from true Christianity
is leading them; and the same interpretation may be
put on the warning against tolerating in the Church
any 'fornicator or profane person like Esau'. It is not
certain that the first of these two terms necessarily refers
to sexual immorality, as Dr. Moffatt thinks, for the
whole context is dominated by the idea of *religious*
infidelity, spiritual lapse from the truth of God: certainly it was unbelief in the divine promise to his house,
not mere sensuality, that led Esau to the irrevocable
step of bartering away his birthright. No later repentance was able to undo that act (xii. 14-17). It is plain
that for the writer to the Hebrews religion (cf. vi. 4-6)
was not a matter only of repenting and obtaining
forgiveness, but of irrevocable commitment of life to a
supernatural end.

We need not follow the writer's injunctions to the
close. It would be natural enough for him to include
in his letter some matters not necessarily connected
with the central point at issue. Yet the various counsels
about hospitality (xiii. 1-3), maintaining the marriage
bond intact (xiii. 4), avoiding avarice (xiii. 5-6), remem-
bering and submitting to Church leaders (xiii. 7, 17),
and keeping up beneficence and charity (xiii. 16) may

well have been intended as warnings against the un-
fortunate consequences of separation and schism within
the Church.

CONCLUSIONS FROM CHAPTER III

We are now in a position to summarise briefly the
conclusions to which the above study of the admonitory
sections of the Epistle has led.

I. The Epistle in its concentration of interest on the
supernal and heavenly end of the Christian calling and
in the particular terms of its emphasis on the exaltation
of Jesus above the Mosaic Law and the Cultus stands
in the direct line of succession to the teaching of
Stephen and the world-mission.

II. The addressees were a minority group in the
Church which was lapsing from the strength and purity
of its eschatological hope, but whether it was a specifically Jewish-Christian minority affected by influences
from the side of Judaism, or some other group tempted
in a different direction, is not absolutely and finally
determinable from the evidence of these admonitory
sections taken alone.

III. All of the admonitory passages, however, are
compatible with the hypothesis of the Jewish-Christian
character of the group, and several of them distinctly
favour that hypothesis rather than any other. It is only
necessary to recall in this connection what has been
said above on ii. 1-5, iii. 1-5, iv. 1-2, vi. 1-2, vi. 4-6,
x. 25, x. 32-39, and xi. 24-28.[1] None of these passages
lends any colour to the idea that the proclivities of the
group lay in the Hellenistic pagan direction. All of
them, on the contrary, acquire heightened point and

[1] See pp. 48 f., 53, 58 f., 62 f., 64, 68 f., 71 f., 79 f. above for the
evidence of these passages.

relevance if we assume the background of the group to have been Jewish.

Thus, to recapitulate the evidence briefly, the insistence of the writer on the authority of Christ as above that of the 'angels' suggests some leaning of the readers to the Law given on Sinai (ii. 1-5), and the same holds, in only a slightly lesser degree, of his emphasis on the glory of Christ as greater than that of the 'faithful' Moses (iii. 1-3). Also the warning given to certain persons that they are 'crucifying' the Son of God for themselves (vi. 4-6) gains additional point if we take the writer to mean that by their lapse from Christian faith these persons are virtually identifying themselves with the position of the Jews towards Christ.

Again, if the allusion to the early ordeal of suffering which the community underwent after its first enlightenment (x. 32 f.) refers to the Claudian measures taken against the Jews of Rome in A.D. 49, it carries with it the inference that the Christians in question were among the first persons converted to the faith of Christ at Rome, and were, therefore, presumably Jews.

So, again, the strong accentuation of Moses' choice and of his preference of 'the reproach of Christ' to his privilege of place at the Egyptian court (xi. 24-28) is excellently explained, as we have seen, if the Christians addressed were conscious of having forfeited through their adherence to Christ the advantages once possessed by them as Jews under the Roman imperial administration.

IV. The fact that nowhere in these sections is there any hint of Gnostic and Hellenistic aberrations of religious belief on the side of the group is capital evidence in the same direction.

CHAPTER IV

THE THEOLOGICAL ARGUMENT OF THE EPISTLE.—I. THE PERSON AND OFFICE OF THE REDEEMER

THE FINALITY OF THE CHRISTIAN REVELATION
(i. 1-2)

God spoke in old time to our fathers through the prophets. It was in manifold and very varied ways. He has now at the close of these days spoken to us through a Son—one whom He has appointed to be the universal Heir.

The Word of God to man in Christ has come as the climax and last stage in the long diversified history of God's communication with His people Israel. The revelation of divine truth in the past came 'through the prophets' and was effected in multiple and various ways, literally 'by many parts and in many forms'. The method was that one part of the truth was delivered at one time, another part at another time. Now one sort of language was employed, now another sort. When the writer speaks of the 'parts' of this divine economy, he may have been thinking of the traditional division of the Old Testament books into the Law, the Prophets, and the Writings, or, going further back into the past, to the period before the books existed, he may have had in mind such an analysis of the primary sources of revelation as we find in the prophetic sum-

mary, Jeremiah xviii. 18: 'Law will not perish from
the priest, nor counsel from the wise, nor the word
from the prophet.' The *torah* of the priests, the
d^ebarim of the prophets, the *hokhmah* of the wise,
these were the ultimate springs of that knowledge of
God in Israel which was finally gathered up into the
Bible. The many 'forms', in turn, will have included
such media of revelation as God's mighty acts in
history, as well as theophanies, visions, auditions,
dreams, signs, oracles, and other intimations of the
divine will granted to the patriarchs or to the prophets.
But all these are now transcended and superseded in
the manifestation made to the world in Jesus, who is
God's supreme and last Word to men.

This revelation through Christ has come 'at the End
—in these days', that is to say, in the final stage or
phase of world-history. The writer brings in the
eschatological note which, as we have seen, rings
through and through his practical warnings to his
readers. With Christ the last hour of time has struck.
The New Age, the eternal, final order, has announced
itself. Jesus is the messenger and instrument not only
of a 'better' salvation than was revealed in the past,
but of an 'eternal' salvation, one having the nature of
eternity in it. The finality of the Christian revelation
is marked not by its temporal incidence alone, but by
the transcendent character of the Person, the rank,
the status, and the authority of Him through whom
and in whom it comes. Here is not a prophet but a
Son, who as the Messiah of God is the Lord of history,
the divinely appointed Inheritor of the ages.

The doctrine of the Person of Christ in the Epistle
thus shows a definitely Jewish Messianic basis and
starting-point, but it reaches far beyond this. In the

ancient Hebrew kingdom, in the days of the multi-
partite and very various revelation through the prophets,
the king of Israel, as the head of the elect people of
God, was the visible representative and pledge to the
nation of the divine blessing, and an instrument of the
saving and sanctifying virtue, energy, and presence of
God in its life. He was, as such, invested with quasi-
divine titles and honours as the anointed 'Son' of God.[1]
When with the deepening of the awareness of God's
holiness and the increasing sense of the nation's sin
which had come through the prophets,[2] the hope of the
divine salvation and righteousness was projected into
a future age, the idea of a righteous king of David's line
who should be the instrument, assurance, and sacrament of God's saving presence with His people was
projected forwards with it. In later Judaism, however,
the title 'Son of God' was allowed to drop out, probably
in consequence of the reaction which had long set in
against language shared by the Hebrews with their
polytheistic Canaanite neighbours.[3] Now in Christianity the conception of the Messiah as the Son of
God has come back, but on a higher level of revelation,
and with immeasurably new force and depth of meaning, through the person, character, and relation to
God the Father, of Jesus. God has spoken to us in a
Son.

THE SIGNIFICANCE OF CHRIST IN REVELATION. THE WISDOM CHRISTOLOGY (i. 3-14)

Through Him also He made the world. He, the radiance
of God's glory and the very expression of His essence,

[1] Psalms ii. 1-9, lxxxix. 19-27, cx. 1-4; Isaiah ix. 6-7, xi. 1-10, etc.
[2] Cf. Isaiah vi. 1-5.   [3] See Aage Bentzen, *Messias* (1948).

the sustainer also of the universe by His word of power, has now, after effecting the purification of our sins, taken His seat at the right hand of the Majesty on high. He has become as much greater than the angels as the Name He has inherited is more excellent than theirs (i. 3-4).

The full range of the significance of Jesus in revelation now appears in a series of predicates which, it is plain, constitute for the author and his readers the *presuppositions* of faith, the foundation-truths of the Christian religion. As such, they appear also in St. Paul [1] and in the Gospel according to John.[2] For the writer to the Hebrews these truths do not need to be demonstrated or explained. They belong to the givenness of the received gospel. The predications which are made with regard to Jesus here are four in number.

I. He is the Messiah, the Son of God, the pre-destined Inheritor of all things (i. 1-2a).

II. He is the Wisdom or Logos of God, through whom God made the worlds, and who upholds them (i. 2b-3a).

III. He has effected the purification of our sins (i. 3b).

IV. He sits at God's right hand, exalted above the angels (i. 3c-4).

To these four articles, which represent the primary substance of the Church's confession of Christ, the writer appends (i. 5-14) a sequence of Scripture proof-texts, nearly all drawn from the Psalms, and carefully arranged to provide point-to-point support for the successive statements. Thus (a) Psalm ii. 7 and

[1] Cf. 1 Corinthians i. 30, viii. 5-6; Colossians i. 14-17.
[2] Cf. i. 1-4, 14, 16-17, etc.

2 Samuel vii. 14 are quoted as evidence for the divine Sonship of Christ, (*b*) Psalm xcvii. 7 (LXX), Psalm civ. 4, and Psalm xlv. 6-7 predicate His supreme rank and Lordship, (*c*) Psalm cii. 25-27 refers to His part in the work of creation, and (*d*) Psalm cx. 1 proclaims His enthronement and exaltation above the angels. No Old Testament passage is quoted at this point in illustration of the priestly function of Christ by which our purification from sin is effected, but throughout the rest of the Epistle Psalm cx. 4 is repeatedly cited for this purpose.

While some of the proof-texts quoted, for example those from Psalms ii., xlv., lxxxix., and cx., are words which in their original context refer directly to the Messianic king of Israel, others like Psalm xcvii. 7 and cii. 25-27 bear on the worship or glory due to God Himself. We must, therefore, conclude that for the Christian author of Hebrews all such passages count now as utterances prophetically relating to Christ in His pre-existent life and status with God. Thus the word in verse 6, 'Let all the angels of God worship Him', which goes back in part to the Septuagint version of Psalm xcvii. 7 and in part to the same version of Deuteronomy xxxii. 43, is understood as a summons to the angels to worship the eternal *Son*. The writer's introduction of the citation is in the form: 'Again, when He brings the Firstborn into the world, He says, Let all the angels, etc.' On the writer's own principles of Old Testament interpretation this is really the equivalent of saying: 'When God says, as He says in the Psalm, Let all the angels of God worship Him, God is speaking of the time when He is to bring the Firstborn, that is, the Messiah, into the world.' In thus thinking of the pre-incarnate Son of God as already present and instant in the word given to Israel and in the history of Israel the author of Hebrews is taking the same ground as is taken by St. Paul and the Fourth Evangelist.

With regard to the aspects of the function of Christ set out in the four great affirmations which have been listed above, the first or Messianic predication proper, according to which Jesus is the divinely predestined and scripturally promised Heir of the ages and Lord of history, has already been considered. It rests upon the Psalms and the prophets. The third or sacrificial aspect of His function will occupy us throughout the later chapters of the Epistle. The fourth, which asserts the superiority of His title and prerogatives with respect to the angels, goes with the first, and will come up again for notice presently. The second of the four predications, according to which the Messianic Son of God is also, in effect, the *Wisdom* or *Logos* of God, through whom the worlds were made and God's invisible being or essence brought to expression, requires further consideration at this point.

The Jewish conception of the Wisdom of God, which is found present and already in semi-poetical course of development in Proverbs viii., especially in verses 22-31, was destined to receive further elaboration in Ecclesiasticus and, under the influence of Greek philosophical thought, in the Alexandrian book of the Wisdom of Solomon. Thus in Proverbs, in the passage referred to, Wisdom is represented as saying:

'The Lord possessed me in the beginning of His way, before His works of old. I was set up from everlasting, from the beginning, before the earth existed. . . . When He marked out the foundations of the earth, then I was by Him as a master workman, and I was daily His delight.'

In Ecclesiasticus xxiv. the same conception is wrought out with special emphasis upon the indwelling and activity of Wisdom in Israel; Wisdom, the pre-cosmic Word of God, the primal Light, was symbolised in the pillar of cloud, and ministered in the holy tabernacle in the beloved city of Jerusalem; she took root among the glorified people of the Lord's inheritance. It is Wisdom that is revealed in the Torah of Israel and in prophecy. In the book of the Wisdom of Solomon vii. 21 ff. the inwardness of the indwelling of this prin-ciple is elaborated by aid of a philosophical terminology borrowed from the Greeks:

'She pervades and penetrates all things by reason of her pureness. For she is a breath of the power of God and a clear effluence of the glory of the Almighty. . . . She is an effulgence from everlasting light, and an unspotted mirror of the working of God, and an image of His goodness. . . . From generation to generation, passing into holy souls, she makes men friends of God and prophets.'

Wisdom, therefore, is personified in these books as the principle of the divine energy and activity in creation and history, the principle also of all communication between God and the spirit of man. When and where the identification or conjunction of this principle with the Messiah-concept first took place cannot be precisely determined. There existed the potentiality of such a conjunction in the promise to the Davidic Messiah of 'the spirit of wisdom and understanding, the spirit of counsel and might, the spirit of knowledge and of the fear of the Lord' (Isaiah xi. 2), and in the endowment of the apocalyptic Son of Man with 'the spirit of wisdom, and the spirit which gives insight, and the spirit of understanding' (1 Enoch xlix. 3). But while there was thus an approach to a combination of the concepts from the side of the Jewish Messiah-idea, strangely enough there was no reciprocal movement from the side of the Jewish Wisdom-theology. There we find that, though in Ecclesiasticus and the Jewish Alexandrian literature Wisdom is identified with the Torah and with the Spirit of God, it is not brought into any relation to the Messiah, for the Messiah has no place in that literature. Philo also, while he gives a wide extension of meaning to the idea of the Logos, and provides this principle with a variety of Old Testament theological titles, such as Son of God, Firstborn, Name of God, Heavenly Man or man in the Image of God, nowhere gives a Messianic sense to these titles or includes in his synthesis the name of the Messiah.[1] On the other hand, in St. Paul, in the Fourth Gospel, and here in the Epistle to the Hebrews, the identification of the Wisdom of God with the Christ of God is as instinctive as it is complete. *We seem warranted, therefore, in concluding that the conjunction of the Messiah-concept and the Wisdom-concept first occurred within the Christian Church, and indeed, as the convergent evidence of St. Paul, Hebrews, and the Johannine literature shows, within the theology of the world-mission.* And there it started, not from any theorisings about the principle of Wisdom, but rather from the revelational value of what had come to the Church in Jesus who as the Messiah or Son of Man, the Lord of all nations, was also the Light of the nations, as prophets

---

[1] For Philo see especially *De Conf. Ling.*, 146.

(Isaiah) and apocalyptists (1 Enoch xlviii. 4) had declared.

In this connection it is to be noticed that, whereas Philo's synthesis of other concepts with the Logos signified the drawing of these concepts over to the side of what was at best a religious-philosophical abstraction, in Christianity the opposite has happened. The abstract semi-philosophical notions of the Wisdom or Logos of God are drawn over to, and absorbed into the personal Christ of the Church's faith, a clear evidence of the superior power and dominating influence of the living spirit of Jesus. In the light of this result we are justified in saying that the Wisdom or Logos conception of Judaism was at best only a Messianic potential, only a prophetical type of the Messiah. It needed a more vital religious impulse than Judaism itself could generate to effect the ultimate synthesis of the conceptions.

It may be added that the Christian identification of Jesus the Messiah with the divine Wisdom or creative Word of God in the Old Testament would be part of the same general process by which He, in whom the eternal world was revealed to faith, was seen as active in the Old Testament history during His *pre-incarnate* life. If, for example, it is the pre-incarnate Son of God who, according to Hebrews x. 5-10, speaks the words 'Lo, I come to do Thy will' in Psalm xl., the same kind of reasoning could ascribe to Him the already quoted words uttered by Wisdom in Proverbs viii. 22 ff. and elsewhere.

In our passage of Hebrews, though the title of Wisdom or Logos is not expressly assigned to Jesus, the Wisdom-derivation of the explicative predicates used to bring out His cosmic significance is quite indubitable. The term 'radiance' or 'effulgence' of the divine glory, for example, repeats an epithet applied to Wisdom in the Wisdom of Solomon vii. 25-26, as we have seen, and the conceptions of Christ as the 'expression' or 'imprint' of God's being and as the instrument of God in creation carry forward elements of the same Alexandrian theology. But in Christianity an immense and endless new significance has been imparted to these terms, as also to the Messianic idea, through their ascription to Jesus as the personal Revealer of God.

We may say, then, that in the course of the earliest development of Christian thought the conception of the Person of Jesus in its significance for religion passed through two stages of expression. In the first of these stages it took to itself the Messianic terminology of Palestinian Judaism, and on the lips both of Jesus and of His followers enunciated itself by the aid of the titles 'Christ', 'Son of God', and 'Son of Man'. Only through such language could the finality of the revelation made in the word and work of Jesus be stated in a form adequate for the purpose and sufficiently related to the history of prophetic religion in the past. Secondly, with the beginnings of the Christian world-mission the Church's proclamation of Jesus took over, in addition, the vocabulary of the Jewish-Alexandrian school of Wisdom-theology. This medium of expression, connecting as it did on the one side with the Old Testament conception of the Word or Torah of God, and on the other side with the Greek idea of the divine Mind or Reason operative in the universe, brought out for the larger world the ultimate nature of the claim made for Jesus in the confession of the Church.

G

THE INCARNATION IN RELATION TO MAN,
SUFFERING, AND SIN (ii. 5-18)

For it is not to the angels that God has subjected the
World to Come, of which we speak. A speaker has in
one place declared himself in these terms: 'What is
man that Thou rememberest him? or the son of man
that Thou payest him any heed? Thou hast made him
for a little time lower than the angels, Thou hast
crowned him with glory and honour, and set him over
the works of Thy hands, Thou hast placed all things
under his feet.' Now, in this placing of 'all things
under him' he has left out nothing that is not so placed.
But, as it is, we do not yet see all things placed under
man. What we see is Jesus. He is 'made for a little
time lower than the angels' in order to suffer death.
He is 'crowned with glory and honour' that by the
grace of God He might experience death on behalf of
every man (ii. 5-9).

The starting-point of the writer's argument has been
the transcendence of Jesus over the angels, who are
the ordainers and custodians of the Jewish Law; but in
thinking of the angels the writer's mind is carried to
Psalm viii., which speaks of man's place with reference
to these celestial beings, and this gives the writer a
chance to speak of Jesus in His relation to men. The
Psalm speaks of 'man' or 'son of man' as having had
conferred on him by God the rank described as only
'a little lower than the angels', and as being 'crowned
with glory and honour' and set over all God's works,
with the whole world placed under his control. Now,
says the writer, this statement does not correspond with
what we see actually taking place in nature and in
history. We do not see man in possession, man as

absolute master of all things in the world. But looking
at Jesus we see the prophecy fulfilled and His supremacy
achieved. Therefore the Psalm relates to Jesus. It is
He, this particular 'Son of Man', who in His incarnate
life is 'made for a little time lower than the angels with
a view to the suffering of death', and who is 'crowned
with glory and honour' that by the grace of God [1] He
might experience death on behalf of universal man.
The writer understands both the humiliation and the
exaltation or coronation of Jesus to have taken place
for the sake of the oblation made on the Cross. The
glory, as well as the humiliation, is for Christian eyes
('we see') already present in the Incarnate Life. Here
two observations fall to be made.

(1) In form, the argument is exactly similar to the
one attributed in Acts ii. 25-36 to the Apostle Peter,
who on the day of Pentecost reasons that, since the
prediction of David in Psalm xvi. 10, 'Thou wilt not
leave my soul to Sheol, nor suffer Thy holy one to see
corruption', was not fulfilled in the case of the patriarch
himself, therefore it is a prophetical reference to Jesus
whom Christians know to be risen from the dead. In
the Hebrews passage the interpretation given to Psalm
viii. establishes the supremacy of Jesus as the Head

---

[1] The reading ' by the grace of God ' in this verse (ii. 9) is that of
all Greek MSS. (except M and 424) and of all ancient Versions (except
three Codices of the Peshitto). It was also apparently the only
reading known to Eusebius, Athanasius, and Chrysostom. But
another reading ' apart from God ', which is found in M and 424,
was known to Origen, Theodoret, Ambrose, Theodore of Mopsuestia,
and Jerome : it was preferred by Origen (who follows it in four out
of six passages in which he cites the verse) and strongly defended
by Theodore. Origen took it to mean that Christ was to taste death
for everyone ' except God '. See Dr. Moffatt's note in his *Commentary*, pp. 26 f. We may agree with Dr. Moffatt that the good
connection of the reading ' by the grace of God ' with the ' It befitted
God ' of the immediately succeeding verse is a point in its favour.

of humanity and the Representative of the race with God.

(2) It is to be noted, as Dr. E. F. Scott points out, that the author's intense interest in this passage is concentrated upon the *suffering* by which, in His identification of Himself with men, the Christ was prepared for His function as our High-Priest in things pertaining to God.[1] Nothing, for example, is said of His teaching, His revelation of the nature and the will of God. We find a similar concentration of interest again where the writer comes to deal with the Old and the New Covenants in chapters viii.-x. The Old Covenant and the Law went together, but the writer's interest in the Law is not in point of its particular commandments— nothing is said, for instance, of circumcision, or of the Sabbath, or of the dietary regulations—but in its design as a whole 'to secure for Israel the right of access to God'. Hence everything is subordinated to the cultus and, in particular, to the priesthood, for it was on the basis of the latter (vii. 11) that the Law was enacted for the people of God.

For it was appropriate that God, He for whom and through whom the whole of things exists, should, in the act of bringing many sons to glory, perfect by suffering the Pioneer of their salvation. The Sanctifier and the sanctified here form a unity. That is the reason for His not being ashamed to call them His brethren when He says 'I will declare Thy name to My brethren, within the Church I will sing to Thee', and again, 'I will be confident in Him', and again, 'Here am I and the children whom God has given Me.' Since the children participate in blood and flesh, He similarly has accepted His share in these, that by dying He might reduce to

[1] *The Epistle to the Hebrews*, pp. 98 f.

impotence him who exercises his sovereignty in death—
that means, the devil—and thereby release all those who
throughout their life were bound like slaves under the
fear of death. Clearly, it is not to the help of the angels
that Jesus comes, but to the help of the race of Abraham.
Obligation was upon Him to be assimilated to His
brethren in every way, and so to become a merciful and
faithful High-Priest in His service of God, in the making
of an expiation for the sins of the people. In the suffering He has Himself sustained under His temptation lies
His power to help those who are tempted (ii. 10-18).

In this supremely great passage the writer, having
in mind what he has just said about the Incarnate Life
of Jesus as revealing, alike in its humiliation and in
its glory, the predestination of the Son of Man to
suffering, speaks of the divine appropriateness of it all.
'It befitted God' that His purpose of redemption—His
act of bringing 'many sons' to the glory of the World
to Come—should plumb the whole depth of human
anguish and death. For the realisation of this right
requirement it was necessary that the 'Son' of God,
who was to be the agent and the 'Pioneer', should in
His own person not only exhibit perfect obedience to
God, but achieve also a perfect identification of Himself
with men, and thus be qualified to be our perfect
Minister with God. The Gospel of St. Matthew speaks
in one passage of what was proper or fitting for Jesus,[1]
and St. Paul repeatedly alludes to what is proper or
fitting for the faithful,[2] but only the writer to the
Hebrews in the New Testament uses this kind of
language with reference to God. When he speaks of the
fitness of God's action, we may recall, however, that

---

[1] Matthew iii. 15.
[2] 1 Corinthians xi. 13, Ephesians v. 3, 1 Timothy ii. 10, Titus ii. 1.

Old Testament prophets are found constantly appealing to God by reference to His own revealed character of righteousness and mercy. They judge God by God, so to speak, and insist on the divine consistency. So here, if what is 'proper' to God comes in as standard of judgment, the approach is not from any idealistically conceived standpoint but from the self-evidence of the revelation of grace granted in Jesus Christ Himself. The God who is so judged, however, is the God of creation and of history, 'from whom and through whom', says the writer, 'the whole of things exists'. The Passion of Jesus, in other words, in which we have the true measure of the divine character, is not irrational or irrelevant with reference to the divine ordering of the world, but is of its very structure and essence. In support of the utter self-identification of Jesus with men, by which the Sanctifier and the sanctified are revealed in their unity, the writer cites a trio of Old Testament passages[1] which once again show that, where psalmists and prophets spoke, the overtones, so to speak, were those of the pre-existent Christ. And here, in speaking of the complete participation of the Incarnate Christ in the 'children's' blood and flesh, the writer comes to something which calls for fuller critical remark and elucidation.

JESUS HERO AND PRIEST

When the writer, in the first verse of the above passage (ii. 10-18), gives to the Son of God the title of 'Pioneer' (*archegos*) or *Bahnbrecher* of our salvation, there slips in the note of what may be definitely called

[1] Psalm xxii. 22, Isaiah viii. 17, 18.

a 'Hero-Christology'.[1] Jesus is conceived as the Leader or Protagonist who, going in front or at the head of His redeemed host, beats down the forces opposed to them, and so becomes the Founder or Inaugurator of their 'salvation'. This conception comes into clear light at the heart of the passage, where it is said that the purpose underlying the assumption by the Son of God of the children's blood and flesh was that He might 'defeat' the devil, who exercised his sovereignty in death, and by that stroke release all those who, like slaves, were cowed and bent low throughout their earthly existence beneath 'the fear of death'.

A form of the same Christology confronts us in St. Paul as, for example, in 1 Corinthians ii. 6-8, where the Apostle writes that 'if the Archons (Rulers, supernaturally conceived) of the present world-order had known the wisdom of God, they would not have crucified the Lord of glory', and thereby subjected themselves to surprise and overthrow. It occurs again more pointedly in Colossians ii. 15, where the Apostle represents Christ on the Cross as 'disarming the Powers and Authorities' and 'making a public spectacle of them, by triumphing over them' on the Cross. A similar Christology is expressed again in the Fourth Gospel in the word (xii. 31): 'The time has come for the judgment of the world, and for the Prince of this world to be expelled; and I, if I am lifted up from the earth, will draw all men to Myself', and in the prediction (xiv. 30): 'The Prince of this world comes, and he has no hold over Me'. In the Synoptic Gospels also the same Christology is present, not only in the narrative

---

[1] Cf. the article by the late Canon Wilfrid L. Knox on ' The Divine Hero Christology in the New Testament ' in *Harvard Theological Review*, October 1948.

of the temptation of the Son of God in the wilderness and in the whole tremendous engagement of Jesus with demonic forces in human life, but in words like 'I beheld Satan fallen like a lightning-brand from heaven' (Luke x. 18), or 'Simon, Satan has asked to have you (all), to sift you (all) like wheat, but I have prayed for thee' (Luke xxii. 31). In the light of this conjunct evidence of St. Paul, the Synoptic Gospels, and the Johannine literature we seem justified in assuming that a type of Hero-Christology, in which Jesus, like a Christian Herakles,[1] is locked in mortal conflict with the powers of darkness and overthrows them by His Cross and Resurrection or, alternatively, is sent by God 'in the likeness of sinful flesh' and condemns sin in the flesh to death (Romans viii. 3), belonged to the primordial substance of the world-mission theology of the Church.

While, however, the writer to the Hebrews also knows it and gives expression to it in the present passage, he does not pursue this line of Christology any further, but immediately diverts the stream of his argument away to the priestly ministry of Jesus. Jesus came to the help of Abraham's race, not of the angels. Yes! He had to be assimilated in every way to His brethren. Yes! But all this was that He might 'become a merciful and faithful *High-Priest* in His service of God, in the making of an expiation for the sins of the people'.

This is the point at which to raise a question of the first critical magnitude. If the writer of this Epistle was addressing not a Jewish-Christian audience but some other undifferentiated group representing the general body of the Church, *why does his Christology*

[1] *Harvard Theological Review*, October 1948, pp. 245 f.

at this point turn so completely and irreversibly in the direction of a hieratical and ritual interpretation of the work of Jesus Christ? If the persons whom the author had in mind were ordinary Hellenistic Christians who were discouraged perhaps because the Lord had not come, and were tempted to lapse into apathy or to fall again to pagan errors, could he not have made capital use of this Hero-Christology which, even if every reference to Greek mythological analogies were ruthlessly expunged, could yet be counted upon to engage subconscious elements in the Greek mind and to awaken new courage and hope? Death overthrown! The powers of hell vanquished! Why does the writer turn so insistently in all that follows of the Epistle to the one subject of Christ as our Priest and of Christ's self-oblation in death as an expiation for our sins? Why this Priest-Christology? Indeed, the question cannot be repressed: Would the author have addressed himself in this way to any other than a Jewish-Christian audience whose full Christian development was being retarded by some kind of sentimental attraction or influence proceeding from the ancient Jewish sacraments of grace?

Admittedly, a pure Hero-Christology would not have satisfied the writer any more than it satisfied St. Paul or the Fourth Evangelist. It would not have brought out *quanti ponderis sit peccatum*. But why does he turn for the fuller elucidation of Christ's function as Redeemer to the institutions of the priesthood and the cultus? We shall have to return to this point presently.

We pass over the section iii. 1-iv. 16, which was considered in the earlier survey of the admonitory material of the Epistle, and come to the central thematic subject of the first half of the work. It should be noticed that already on two occasions (ii. 17-18 and iv. 14-16) the author has led his argument up by deliberate stages to the High-Priesthood of Jesus.

PRIEST BY PREDESTINATION AND INCARNATE QUALIFICATION (v. 1-10)

For every high-priest who is taken from the ranks of men is appointed to act on behalf of men in their relations with God. It is that he may offer gifts and sacrifices for sins. He is one who can bear gently with the ignorant and erring, since he too in himself is beset with weakness: and for this reason too he is obliged to present sin-offerings for himself as well as for the people. Moreover, no one takes the office to himself, but (only as he is) called to it by God, as Aaron was. So also the Christ did not by any self-glorification attain to His High-Priesthood. It was God saying to Him, 'Thou art My Son, I have this day begotten Thee', just as in another place He says, 'Thou art a priest for ever, after the order of Melchisedek' (v. 1-6).

The ordinances for the high-priest in the religion of Israel were intended, as Dr. E. F. Scott says, 'to illuminate the nature of that higher ministry whereby the true access to God could at last be realised'.[1] With the observance of the provisions for the priesthood and the sacrifices, as with the ordinances for the king and the royal supremacy, the Divine Blessing, the virtue, energy, power, and presence of God with His people were bound up. These could only exist and operate in Israel as the ceremonial purity of the nation was maintained or, when lost, restored. But it is not just to say that the writer to the Hebrews, in making use

[1] *The Epistle to the Hebrews*, p. 123 f.

of these ancient ideas, is attempting to pour new wine into old bottles and is confusing the character of the Christian religion by appeal to outworn ceremonies and institutions. As Dr. Scott himself acknowledges, the writer's attention to the details of the Old Testament regulations throughout the Epistle is neither thorough nor exact, and this suggests that the starting-point and basis of his interest is not the old ritual but Christ. Certainly it is not a case of his pouring the new wine into old containers, but, on the contrary, he absorbs the old types and ordinances into Christ's fulfilment of them.

No comment is needed on the passage v. 1-10 except that the author, in citing the analogy of the Aaronic priesthood, stresses its inward side and its divine call rather than its titular privilege as derived by family lineage. According to the Law on the latter point, 'no stranger, who is not of the seed of Aaron, may come near to burn incense before the Lord' (Numbers xvi. 40); nevertheless the divine call operates in this legislation, and a moral urgency existed in Israel that the priest should be inwardly conformed to the nature of his office. His liturgical function to offer gifts and sacrifices for sins morally presupposes in him the capacity in some sense to take the sins and frailties of men upon himself. His sense of his oneness with men in weakness and need is kept alive by the continuous obligation (Leviticus ix. 7, xvi. 17) to make atonement-offerings for himself as well as for the commonwealth of Israel. Nor must it be forgotten that the same compulsion lies at the heart of his other essential function, his didactic office as giver to Israel of the Torah of God, though the writer does not here or else-where allude to this task as appertaining either to the priest or to Jesus.[1] His sympathetic and inward presentation of the priesthood in Israel is, nevertheless, to be noted, and it may well owe its essential character to the writer's profound insight into the Saviour's vicarious relation to sinful and suffering men. The writer is one who has meditated on the character of Christ as Priest, and so has been led to see what all ministerial priesthood, in its own place, is intended to be.

His analysis of the divine call of the Saviour is into the two elements, derived from the Messianic Psalms of Israel:

'Thou art my Son' (Psalm ii. 7).

'Thou art a Priest for ever, after the order of Melchizedek' (Psalm cx. 4).

The fact that the writer is not content to express the Saviour's mission in terms of Psalm ii. 7 alone shows that neither a pure Hero-Christology nor a merely spiritual Filial-Christology such as might have been drawn out of that Psalm would have satisfied him. Nevertheless, the recognition that some addition was necessary does not of itself explain why the particular addendum should be taken from Psalm cx. The voice 'Thou art My Son' is attested by the Synoptic tradition.[2] Is it not possible that the other voice, 'Thou art a Priest for ever', was also a part of the primitive tradition of the world-mission, though the written Gospels do not attest it?

It is contended by Dr. E. F. Scott, indeed, that the doctrine of the Priesthood of Christ in the Epistle represents a new and individual feature in the writer's

---

[1] On the priesthood of Israel and its teaching function see Pedersen's *Israel*, III-IV, pp. 150-197, especially 160-164.
[2] Mark i. 11, ix. 7; Matthew iv. 3, 6, etc.

theology, not a remoulding of traditional ideas. But it is difficult to sustain this judgment in the face of the 110th Psalm, and in the face also of such other facts as that in Maccabean times a Messiah from the house of Levi was expected, and that the Zadokite party which sprang up within the priesthood in the second century before Christ expected the advent of a Messiah 'from Aaron and Israel'.[1]

In the days of His flesh, He brought prayers and supplications with passionate cries and tears to Him who was able to save Him from death, and because of His godliness He was heard. Thus, though Son, He learned obedience through the things He suffered, and being thereby perfected, He has become in His person the source of an eternal salvation for all who obey Him, with the title from God of ' High-Priest after the order of Melchizedek ' (v. 7-10).

The purpose of these moving words, which sound the very depths of the writer's reflection on the spiritual drama of the life of Jesus, is to show how intensely Jesus entered into the human lot. It was this experience that wrung from Him His prayers and entreaties, cries and tears; for man is born unto trouble as the sparks fly upwards. 'No theoretical reflection on the qualification of priests or upon the dogma of Messiah's sinlessness', writes Dr. Moffatt, 'could have produced such passages as this.'[2] But while that is true, it may have been the dwelling of his mind on the character of the Saviour as *Priest* that made the writer to the Hebrews more sensitive to this side of the human story

---

[1] See R. H. Charles, 'Fragments of a Zadokite Work' in *Apocrypha and Pseudepigrapha of the Old Testament*, II. pp. 785 and 795 f.

[2] *Commentary* on the passage.

of Jesus than any other writer in the New Testament.
He has before his mind the agony of Jesus in the Garden
of Gethsemane or some tradition of His words resembling that which comes to expression in the Fourth
Gospel:

> ' Now is My soul troubled, and what shall I say?
>   " Father, save Me from this hour ? "
> Nay, I have come to this hour for this cause.
>   " Father, glorify Thy name " ! '

Such traditions, illustrating at once the stress and
anguish of Jesus and His 'reverence' for God, were
carried at the heart of the world-mission of Christianity,
for it was out of the preaching and teaching of the
world-mission that the Gospels arose. The writer will,
by appeal to this soul-travail, show us what it was for
Jesus to be a Son, and what it was to be a Priest, and
what it was to be both of these things together. 'He
learned obedience by the things He suffered', thus
supremely illustrating in His person the truth of the
Greek adage immortally expressed in the famous lines
of Aeschylus:

> By Zeus in heaven,
> Who set us mortals on the road of thought,
>   Was the rule given—
> 'Wisdom by suffering must for man be wrought!'
>   This a compelling grace man owns
> Of heavenly Spirits on their august Thrones.[1]

Nor can there be any doubt that for the writer the suffering, the prayers, and the cries of Jesus were part of the
sacrificial Oblation by which the obedient Son of God
became also for us the perfectly qualified Priest, the
author of a salvation having the nature of eternity in it.
No demonstration could be clearer of the place which

[1] *Agamemnon*, 176 ff.

the human life of Jesus has in the Christology of the Epistle to the Hebrews. As Dr. E. F. Scott observes, there is no refusal here to know Christ 'after the flesh', as in 2 Corinthians v. 16: no discrimination of any essential kind between a first manifestation of the Son of God after the flesh and a second post-Resurrection stadium in which the manifestation is 'after the Spirit of holiness', as in Romans i. 3-4. Nor are the human attributes of Jesus visibly pervaded and penetrated at every point, as in the Fourth Gospel, by the divine. It is a real Incarnation which is described in Hebrews. The Passion of the Saviour is apprehended in the deeply emotional character of His human experience, and 'in words of exquisite feeling' is presented for the response of feeling on our part. In this respect, as Dr. Scott recognises, the Epistle to the Hebrews comes nearer to modern sentiment than, perhaps, any book in the New Testament.[1]

We pass over the section v. 11-vi. 20, which has been considered in another connection.

PRIEST AFTER THE ORDER OF MELCHIZEDEK. PRIEST OF THE RESURRECTION (vii. 1-28)

The writer will now show that the predestination of Jesus the Messiah to Priesthood after the order of Melchizedek (Psalm cx. 4) of necessity carries with it the supersession of the Aaronic priesthood together with the Law and the Covenant, with which that priesthood stood in indissoluble historical relation.

For this Melchizedek, king of Salem, priest of the Most High God, who met Abraham as he returned from the slaughter of the kings and blessed him, and to whom

[1] *The Epistle to the Hebrews*, pp. 149 f.

Abraham on his part apportioned a tenth of everything, is first, as the translation of his name shows, king of righteousness, and then king of Salem, which means king of peace. He has no father, no mother, no genealogy: he has neither a beginning to his days, nor an end to his life, but, (herein) resembling the Son of God, he continues as a priest for ever (vii. 1-3).

The starting-point of the Christian writer is, of course, Psalm cx. 4, but in order to develop the mystical overtones of the declaration in that Messianic Psalm he goes back to the Melchizedek-passage in Genesis xiv. 18-20, and constructs a *midrash* upon it. The Genesis-narrative recorded simply that, after Abraham's return from the slaughter of Chedorlaomer and the confederate kings, Melchizedek, the king of Salem, met him with bread and wine, that he was priest of 'El 'Elyon (God Most High), that he blessed Abraham in the name of 'El 'Elyon and blessed 'El 'Elyon for the victory given to Abraham, and that Abraham gave Melchizedek a tenth of everything. The writer to the Hebrews takes no account of the bread and wine which Melchizedek offered—an omission which we shall have occasion to notice at a later point—but mentions that Melchizedek was king of Salem and priest of the Most High God, that he blessed Abraham, and that Abraham gave him the tithe. For the rest, the writer takes advantage of the absence from the Genesis-narrative of all reference to Melchizedek's parentage—a thing unusual in Semitic records—as well as to his birth and death, and presents the king of Salem as without father or mother or genealogy, and as having no beginning to his days or end to his life. By this exegetical *tour de force* he succeeds in differentiating Melchizedek's type of priesthood from the Aaronic, which depended on genealogy and succession and was subject to mortality. At the same time he contrives to throw over Melchizedek an *aura* of mystery by which the priest of Salem becomes a symbol of the heavenly or eternal priesthood of Christ. The statement, however, that Melchizedek was in this matter 'assimilated to the Son of God' should be limited, in its range of application, to the one particular point that he 'remains a priest for ever', that is, he has no successor. If we press the analogy further, we get into theological difficulties, as the history of patristic exegesis shows.[1]

In the succeeding passage (vii. 4-10) the dignity of Melchizedek is brought out by the fact that he even tithed Abraham. He blessed Abraham, the bearer of the divine promise, and 'incontrovertibly it is the less who is blessed by the greater'. In addition, when he tithed Abraham, he who had himself no place in the Levitical line was already, in effect, tithing Levi, Abraham's unborn descendant. The sons of Levi, the legal receivers of the tithe in Israel, who are 'mortal men', were thus placed in subordination to a priest of whom it is deponed (Psalm cx. 4) that 'he lives'.

Why should the writer labour points like these, unless he were writing to some over whom the official ordinances of Judaism, if not the hierarchy, still cast a spell?

Now, if perfection had been possible through the Levitical priesthood—it is on the basis of that priesthood that the people had been given the Law—what further need was there for another priest to arise 'after the order of Melchizedek', instead of being described as after the order of Aaron? For, when the priesthood is

[1] For this history see the interesting and instructive note of Dr. Moffatt, *Commentary*, p. 93.

H

altered, there necessarily occurs an alteration of the Law as well. Well, He of whom these things are spoken has had His lineage from another tribe from which no one has ever acceded to the altar. It is quite plain that our Lord has arisen out of Judah, and Moses has not said a word about priests with reference to that tribe. And the evidence becomes more transparent still when that other priest arises after ' the likeness of Melchizedek', as one who has become priest, not by the law of a physical requirement, but in virtue of an indissoluble life. The witness which is borne to Him is, 'Thou art a priest for ever, after the order of Melchizedek'. Here comes in the abrogation of an earlier ordinance on account of its weakness and uselessness (for the Law brought nothing to perfection), and the introduction of a superior hope, through which we draw near to God (vii. 11-19).

We have now the central pivotal idea on which the great thematic argument of the writer turns, so far as it concerns the authority of Jesus Christ in revealed religion. The new priesthood implies that the old Law and, as we shall see, the Old Covenant are abrogated. And here, especially in the two closing verses of the section, the parallelism of the writer's theology and St. Paul's becomes exceedingly close. St. Paul and the Epistle to the Hebrews arrive at the same conclusion, namely, that the Law is superseded and abrogated through Christ, but they come to it by different roads. St. Paul's argument is an ellipse having two focal centres: (a) the promise of God to Abraham came before the Law of Moses, and was not annulled by the Law (Galatians iii. 17); (b) if the Law had had the power to communicate life, rightness with God would have come to us through it (Galatians iii. 21). The argument of Hebrews, in turn, has as focal centres these: (*a*) the higher priesthood of Melchizedek was announced to Abraham before the Levitical priesthood existed, and its 'order is not cancelled by the latter; (*b*) if 'perfection', the complete facilitation of our approach to God, had been possible through the Levitical priesthood, no other priest, such as the one predicted in Psalm cx. 4, would have arisen. In St. Paul the abrogation of the Law as a source of rightness with God implicitly carries the fall of the cultus with it. In Hebrews the supersession of the cultus explicitly involves the repeal of the Law. The Epistle thus supplements the Pauline argument at a point which St. Paul had left untouched, but which was of very great importance and interest to the world-mission. For who shall say that a less urgent practical necessity dictated the course of this writer's 'word of exhortation' to his Roman readers than dictated the letter of St. Paul to the Galatians?

There is indeed a difference, here as elsewhere, in the attitudes of St. Paul and the author of Hebrews to the past. St. Paul cannot think of Christ without having in mind the paradoxical relation in which the Christian salvation stands to Jewish expectation: a crucified Messiah is to the Jews a *skandalon*! The writer to the Hebrews, on the other hand, cannot get away from the positive relation in which the Jewish system of religion stands to Jesus Christ. There is no intellectual *skandalon* in his doctrine, but only a moral one; Christ suffered for us 'without the gate'! Yet for Hebrews, as well as for St. Paul, the Jewish past is a *past*. We have entered through Jesus into a higher order of grace than was made known in Judaism. The difference in the thought of the two writers may be put thus: while St. Paul gets in Christianity what Judaism could not give, the writer to the Hebrews sees himself pointed forward in Judaism to the supernal reality of the grace revealed in Christ, a grace foreshadowed, but only foreshadowed, in the older religion.

We seem, then, to penetrate by the aid of the Epistle to the Hebrews to a stage or phase in the evolution of the early world-mission when at one centre certainly, at other centres very probably, Judaism in its ritual aspect still exercised some kind of spell over the minds of a section of the Christian society.[1] It is perhaps with this fact in mind that the writer to the Hebrews emphasises as the supreme characteristic of Christ's office that He is Priest 'not by the law of a physical commandment, but in virtue of an indissoluble life'. He is appealing here to the Resurrection. Just as St. Paul cannot think of faith except as faith in the God of the Resurrection,[2] so for the writer to the Hebrews Jesus is *Priest of the Resurrection* and the inaugurator of a 'better' hope by which we draw near to God. To this the section vii. 20-25 adds only a number of details, and calls for no comment, except as concerns the moving touch in verse 25, that the Saviour's indissoluble life is given to intercession for those who through Him draw near to God. 'The function of intercession in heaven for the People', says Dr. Moffatt, 'which originally was the prerogative of Michael, the angelic guardian of Israel, or generally of angels, is thus transferred to Jesus, to One who is no mere angel, but who has sacrificed Himself for the People.'[3]

Such was the High-Priest suited to our need, holy, innocent, spotless, placed in a different class from sinful

[1] See above, Chapter II, pp. 42 ff.
[2] See especially Romans iv. 19-25, x. 8-9.
[3] *Commentary* on vii. 25. See same work, p. xxxix and note on i. 14. Cf. also p. 51 above.

men, and now made higher than the heavens. He does not need, from day to day, to offer sacrifices, as the high-priests did, first for their own sins, then for those of the people. He has done this once for all by the offering of Himself. For whereas the Law appoints as high-priests men beset with weakness, the word of the Oath, which came after the Law (Psalm cx. 4), appoints a Son who has been perfected for ever (vii. 26-28).

Jesus comes to us from the side of God, but in His perfect holiness of life, character, and function He is the Priest, the Mediator with God, whom our need requires. If it 'befitted' God to make the Hero-prince of our salvation perfect through sufferings (ii. 10), it 'befitted' Jesus as our Priest to make to God the perfect offering of His life. The qualities here attributed to Jesus are not to be understood as passive or negative, but positive and dynamic. They are not merely light but fire. 'In a class apart from sinners' must be taken in this sense, as indicating the completeness of the Saviour's vicarious sacrifice for men. The 'Once-for-allness' of the offering goes with the utter completeness of it. And with this reference to the Saviour's Oblation the writer passes to a new stage of his argument and to a higher plane.

Psalm CX

The survey we have now concluded will have made plain the extent to which the Epistle to the Hebrews is dominated by one great Old Testament oracle— Psalm cx. Here, in verses 1 and 4 combined, we have, as far as Old Testament prophecy can provide it, the charter-document of the writer's Christology, and for him the provision is absolute. Here is *the word of the*

Oath, which, pointing to the advent of the 'better hope through which we draw near to God' (vii. 19-22), announces the Eternal Order which supersedes the Law (vii. 28). Here is also an integral part of the primary Christian *confession* (iii. 1, iv. 14). In view of the frequency with which this Psalm appears and re-appears in Hebrews, like the sun's light seen through trees, it is idle to put down the doctrine of Christ's eternal High-Priesthood to 'a flash of inspiration' on the part of the writer, or to 'a gnosis' to which he has come, an ingenious mental exercise of the order of Philo's speculations on the Logos, a Biblical student's lucubrations on the Old Testament hierarchy. The truth for him was written on the sky. The 110th Psalm exercised a great influence on the primitive Christian mind, and verse 4 was a part of that Psalm.

A generation or two ago, it was customary in certain quarters to connect this King-Priest Psalm with Maccabean times, and even to see in it an ode in celebration of the institution of Simon Maccabeus or his successor, John Hyrcanus, in the dual office of Jewish prince and chief priest. That wave of confidence has passed—it was indeed difficult to account for the entrance of Melchizedek into the Psalm on this hypothesis—and today there is a readier disposition to put the Psalm back to the times of the Israelite monarchy, and to include it in the group of Royal or Enthronement Psalms (ii., xlv. and others) which played a part in some festival-ritual of the Hebrew period. The general thought inspiring these Psalms is that, while God is enthroned over Israel, David or the king of Israel for the time being is His vice-gerent. As for the Melchizedek feature in Psalm cx., it may be suggested that it had its root in a tradition going back in Israel to

the time of David's capture of Zion from the Jebusites
(2 Samuel v. 4-10), when the Hebrew prince succeeded
to prerogatives, political and religious, which had
appertained—compare Genesis xiv. 18—to the Jebusite
sheikhs. On this hypothesis we should be able to
explain the interest which led to the incorporation of
the Melchizedek narrative in Genesis, and, in turn, to
the ascription to the Messianic king in Israel of priesthood 'after the order of Melchizedek', that is to say,
in succession to Melchizedek.

However that may be, the Psalm gives a very instructive portrayal of the powers and prestige, under
God, of the king of Israel. There in succession we find
the enthronement of the king as the representative of
God and of God's righteous reign (verse 1), his investi-
ture with the sceptre of power (verse 2), the acclaiming
homage of his subjects (verse 3), the oath of God con-
firming him 'for ever' (i.e. with his successors) in the
Melchizedek-priesthood in Zion, his victory over the
kings and nations opposed to God (verses 5-6), and his
refreshment from (providential? sacramental?) springs
of life (verse 7).[1]

There were undoubtedly, besides this Psalm, other
influences which helped to set the stage for the development of the Christ-Priest conception in the mind of the
writer to the Hebrews. The reader may here profitably
consult Dr. Moffatt's treatment of the question in his
Commentary.[2] On the one hand, Jewish apocalyptic
literature of the second and first centuries before Christ
had built up the conception of a heavenly world with a
sanctuary and an altar, which formed the 'patterns'
and were thought of as the originals of their earthly

---

[1] See A. Bentzen, *Messias* (1948), pp. 19 f.
[2] Introduction, pp. xlvi-xlix, etc.

counterparts. Dr. R. H. Charles refers to Exodus
xxv. 9, 40 and Numbers viii. 4 as the Scriptural basis
of this idea.[1] Later Judaism, however, did not include
in the picture the conception of a heavenly Priest. It
descried the temple and the altar not made with hands,
but the priest's place was vacant. Judaism felt the need
of the functions of heavenly intercession and expiation,
but it assigned these functions to Michael and the
angels.[2]

Philo, again, has much to say of the Logos as High-
Priest, but it is with the Logos that his thought is really
occupied, not with the Priest. The concrete figure of
the Jewish hierarch is swallowed up in the abstractness
of a philosophical idea. Philo finds support for his
conception in a Pentateuchal passage: 'And there shall
be no man in the tent of meeting when he (the high-
priest) goes in to make atonement in the holy place'
(Leviticus xvi. 17). The Septuagint version, which
Philo follows, runs: 'When the high-priest goes into
the holy of holies, there shall be no man.' This is read
by Philo as meaning that the high-priest in his atone-
ment-making function is not 'man'; he is 'an intermediate nature' between man and God.[3] It is plain
that Philo's high-priest is here drawn into the circle
of abstract conceptions constituting the nature of the
Logos. The Alexandrian theologian, again, has very
little to say about Melchizedek. The latter he describes
as a 'priest-logos, who has as his portion Him who is'.[4]
He is 'one who has attained to a priesthood self-schooled
and self-taught'.[5] The high-priest, upon a really
scientific view directed to the hidden meaning of things,

[1] *The Testaments of the Twelve Patriarchs*, p. 33.
[2] See above, pp. 51 and 116.   [3] *De Somniis*, II. 28.
[4] *Leg. Alleg.*, III. 82.   [5] *De Congressu*, 99.

is, he says, 'not man, but divine Logos'.[1] It can hardly be said, therefore, that Philo stands very directly in the line from which the Christology of Hebrews is descended. In its form the thought of the writer of Hebrews is derived from Psalm cx.: in its matter it derives entirely from the passionate, wholly vicarious life and death of Jesus the Messiah.

[1] *De Fuga*, 108.

CHAPTER V

THE THEOLOGICAL ARGUMENT OF THE EPISTLE.—II. THE OBLATION OF THE BODY OF CHRIST

PRIEST IN THE HEAVENLY SANCTUARY
(viii. 1-6)

A NEW section of the Epistle opens at this point, and runs from viii. 1 to x. 18. Melchizedek disappears. Three new elements enter into the representation. These are (1) the self-offering of Christ or, to speak more exactly, the sacrificial offering of the 'body' of Christ, (2) the heavenly 'sanctuary' in which the Redeemer makes His offering, together with the sustained counterpoint of earthly shadow and heavenly reality which now becomes a feature of the exposition, (3) the new 'covenant', to which Christ's action in the heavenly sphere is relative, and under which the old liturgical order is done away.

So new is the trend and character of the argument that it might at first sight appear that this section was composed in complete independence of the previous train of thought which has centred in Melchizedek and the 110th Psalm. On a closer view, however, the section reveals itself as the natural and indispensable complement of the preceding chapters, presenting as it does the consummation of the ministry of Jesus.

Dr. Moffatt translates the opening words of the section in the form: 'The point of all this is, We do have such a high-priest, one who is seated at the right hand of the throne of Majesty in the heavens, etc.' I do not feel that this rendering does justice at this point to the writer's train of thought, nor to the heightened elevation of the stage to which the argument ascends. While the opening Greek word (*kephalaion*) may mean 'sum' or 'gist' or 'point', to render it here in the form, 'the point of all this is', throws us too much back on the past course of the argument, and fails to bring out the transcendent character of the vista which here opens to our eyes. I would prefer, therefore, to take the word in another of its senses, and to translate:

And now to crown the argument, the High-Priest whom we have is one who has taken His seat at the right hand of the throne of Majesty in heaven, a minister in the Sanctuary or true Tabernacle which the Lord, not man, has fixed (viii. 1-2).

Everything turns at this point on our eyes being directed upwards to the supernal world where at the heavenly altar our Lord is seen presenting His eternal offering. The days of His flesh with their prayers and tears and perfection wrought out in the school of suffering (v. 7-8) are over, and Jesus puts into effect the eternal salvation of which He has become the source (v. 9). Here there comes into view a vision of life on two levels, terrestrial shadow and heavenly substance. It is introduced by the writer's reference to the 'true' sanctuary established not by human hands but by God. Some attention must now, therefore, be given to this 'Alexandrianism' of the Epistle to the Hebrews, a feature which has not seldom been mis-appraised.

The idea of a heavenly sanctuary, with a ritual or worship to correspond, took its start, as we have

noticed, from the Biblical passages, Numbers viii. 4
and Exodus xxv. 9, 40, which speak of the 'pattern'
revealed to Moses on Mount Sinai. But it could call
to its support rich and suggestive material from the
prophets and the Psalms, as where, for example, the
angels or host of heaven are summoned to worship their
Creator and Lord. Dr. R. H. Charles gives it as his
considered judgment that the idea of a sacrificial worship in heaven had long been familiar in Judaism, and
he cites by way of evidence the passage Testament
of Levi iii. 5, where, in the sixth heaven, archangels or
angels of the Presence are said to 'minister and make
propitiation to the Lord for all the ignorance-sins of
the righteous'.[1] This parallelism of the earthly and the
heavenly levels of existence was capable of indefinite
extension, and at Alexandria, where especially the Old
Testament theology was brought into contact with the
Platonism and Stoicism of the eclectic philosophy of
the Hellenistic world, the idea of the heavenly originals
or counterparts of terrestrial things supplied a new
language for the expression of the Biblical doctrine of
the divine creation of the world. Plato's doctrine of
ideas, especially in the form and setting given to it in
the *Timaeus*, was combined with Jewish midrashic
traditions to produce a philosophical and highly edi-
fying exegesis of the books of Moses, especially Genesis.
We find imposing examples in Philo's treatises *De
Opificio Mundi*, the *Legum Allegoriae*, and indeed
passim.[2] But while it is right to see in the Alexandrian
Jewish theology the background against which the
conception of the Two Worlds in the Epistle to the
Hebrews is elaborated, it has to be carefully observed

---

[1] See above, pp. 51 and 116.
[2] For a short statement see *De Opif. Mund.*, 16.

that the interests of the writer to the Hebrews are not in cosmology but in redemption, and that his exposition of the heavenly sanctuary is put into entire subservience to his exposition of the sacrifice and atoning work of Jesus within the Veil. The element of Alexandrianism does not enter into the Epistle until this point is reached, and it is not continued after this point is passed.

Not the nature of reality, but the advent of the End is the dominating concern of the writer. For him the eternal world stands essentially in front of us, *impending* on us as immediate apocalyptic event, and if he brings in the idea of its present heavenly circumstance, it is because Jesus has already gone into the world of light as our 'Forerunner'. He has placed the 'anchor' of our souls there on the other side of the 'veil'. He atones and intercedes for us there, and our souls are summoned to rise to the full height of their eschatological calling.

The fact that the symbolism of the writer is wrought out only in the sphere of 'ritual institutions' is rightly pointed out by Dr. E. F. Scott, who also recognises that for him the earthly shadows of the heavenly things are not deceptive or misleading in their nature, but only imperfect and incomplete. They are not contradicted by their heavenly counterparts, but fulfilled or consummated. Hence the centrality in Hebrews of the notion of 'perfection' (*teleiosis*), the completion or realisation of things which have been here begun.[1] On the other hand, it is plain from the whole character of the Epistle that the writer's interest in the symbolism springs, not from the constitution of his mind, as Dr. Scott considers, nor from any philosophical bias, but from the intensity of his futurist expectation, and

[1] *The Epistle to the Hebrews*, pp. 83 f.

here he is with the Apostles rather than with the idealists.

And because every high-priest is appointed to bring gifts and sacrifices, He must necessarily have some offering to make. Now, if He were on earth, He would not be a priest at all. There are priests there to offer the gifts which the Law requires, (priests) who serve what is only the sketch or shadow-shape of the things in heaven. This accords with the instruction given to Moses when he was about to carry out the building of the tabernacle: 'Look', God says, 'that you make everything after the pattern which was displayed to you on the mountain.' But, as it is, the ministry which Jesus has received is a more excellent one, and He is proportionately the mediator of a better covenant, which has been enacted on the basis of better promises (viii. 3-6).

It is here stated by the writer, in a manner which places the point beyond ambiguity, that the priesthood of the Messiah, declared in Psalm cx., is not an earthly priesthood, but a priesthood in the heavenly realm. The qualification of Jesus for the office, the perfecting of His person as priest, had to be made on earth, but His actual 'liturgy', His ministry of sacrifice, is a transcendent one, and belongs to the New Covenant, of which it is the mark. In the fundamental Biblical pronouncement on the subject the New Covenant is declared to be not as the Old. Jesus is the mediator of a better covenant enacted on a foundation of better promises. In the Epistle the words 'better' and 'eternal' go together in their application to the Christian realities. The latter are better than the former because they have the nature of eternity in them. The eternal world has become actual in them.

THE NEW COVENANT
(viii. 7-13)

The word Covenant has not hitherto appeared in the Epistle except in one anticipatory allusion towards the close of the first half of the work (vii. 22). From this point onwards the term occurs no fewer than sixteen times.

The charter-passage for the New Covenant (Jeremiah xxxi. 31-34) is quoted in full by the writer,[1] and serves as the frontispiece to the second half of the Epistle. The New Covenant itself belongs to, and marks the New Age inaugurated by the entrance of the Redeemer into the heavenly sanctuary, and it forms the framework and setting, as well as the pre-supposition, of all that now follows. The idea of a renovation of the covenant-relation with God was part of that projection of the divine salvation into the future which came about in Israel through the deepening consciousness, produced by the prophets, of the holiness of God. The shadow of national sin had descended heavily on conscience.[2] Righteousness was no longer felt to exist under the existing order. A question-mark had affixed itself to all the institutions, political and sacral, of the nation's life. Not even the charter on which Israel's relation with God was based seemed immune from criticism. Under this general lowering of the lights the vision of a time when God's presence with His people and God's salvation of His people would be unequivocally manifested, inwardly and outwardly, glowed and burned

---

[1] From the Septuagint, and in substantial agreement with the A text.
[2] Cf. especially Isaiah vi. 1-5.

on the prophetic horizon. The Old Covenant stood indicted, but this itself was through the very pressure of the divine word within the prophetic soul. So the writer to the Hebrews understands the prophet Jeremiah.

For had the first covenant been faultless, no place would have been sought for a second. But (it was not so, for) God does find fault with the people, and says: ' See, the days are coming when I will conclude a new covenant with the house of Israel and with the house of Judah ' (viii. 7-8).

The Old Covenant dated from the Exodus, and signalised the redemption of Israel out of Egypt. If the New Covenant is to be different, it is because it will follow upon a new Exodus. But the stress of the prophetic teaching and the reason which it gives for the replacement of the former Covenant by another rests on the past failure of Israel to observe the conditions of the relation formerly entered into with God. Under the new order God's people will be different. They will be inwardly established in the Law and knowledge of God. Above all, God will be merciful to their iniquities and will remember their sins no more. This, for the writer to the Hebrews, represents the climactic element of interest in the new order of grace, for, as Dr. Moffatt observes, it is this divine amnesty, this promise of full and free forgiveness, that is singled out as the high point of the New Covenant when the writer returns to the theme in chapter x. 16-18. Did the writer feel that the supreme defect of the old order was the inefficacy of its means of grace to remove the guilt of sin? Very possibly, but let there be no misunderstanding as to his attitude. *The inadequacy of the cultus was not due to its being a sacrificial system. It was due to its sacrificial system being imperfect.* If the old order is replaced, if, as the writer says,

God has made the first covenant obsolete, and what is obsolete and senescent is on the point of disappearing (viii. 13),

it is not because something of another kind is now being substituted for the sacrifices, but because the latter are to be fully and for ever fulfilled in one transcendent Oblation.

This is a point at which a palpable difference may be observed between the Epistle to the Hebrews and the teaching of St. Paul. For the latter the distinction between the new spiritual Israel and the old Israel is as real as that between the spirit and the flesh. There is not this difference of principle between the respective systems of religion in Hebrews. The author's counterpoint of earthly and heavenly reality does not run out into an opposition of spirit and not-spirit, and it works not a paradox of the orders but an ultimate harmony. Christ transcends, but He also fulfils the religion of Israel. May we not say that St. Paul was led to his particular formulation of the relationship of the two orders by his crucial experience of the Law? He looks at the two in the light of this experience. And for this reason there is a constant sense in him of the crisis and transformation created for all human thought and action by Christ which does not come to expression in the Epistle to the Hebrews.[1]

---

[1] For St. Paul's sense of the antithesis of the new and the old orders at this point cf. Galatians iv. 21-31, 2 Corinthians iii. 15-18, etc.

I

The Old and the New Sanctuaries and their Atonement-Provisions (ix. 1-10)

It is interesting that the writer tests the Old Covenant purely and exclusively by reference to its cultus-provisions. The old order had its means of grace which were designed and offered for the enablement of man's approach to God.

The first covenant had indeed its ordinances of worship and its own material shrine (ix. 1).

'Cosmic' the writer calls the shrine because it belonged to the visible world, which in the language of Alexandria was contrasted with the immaterial or heavenly world. Into the archaeology of his description of the earthly shrine—the outer tent with its furniture, the veil, the inner tent of the most holy place with its sacred objects including the *Hilasterion* or Mercy-Seat (ix. 2-5)—we need not here enter, the less so as the writer declares his account to be at best a summary one (ix. 5). The questions which arise with regard to the correctness of this or that detail in the representation do not specially concern us for the purposes of our argument,[1] but there is one general question which may not be dismissed. That is the overhead question whether the writer would at this point have entered into a discussion of such details if he were not writing to a circle with a definitely Jewish background and with not only a knowledge of, but a sentimental leaning towards the ancient cultus. His main interest, indeed, is concentrated on the one point of the high-priest's office on the Day of Atone-

---

[1] On these questions see Dr. Moffatt's *Commentary ad locum,* and the rich collection of Rabbinical material in Strack-Billerbeck, III. pp. 704-733.

ment, but this itself raises the question: Was a specific interest in the Jewish Day of Atonement a central element in the appeal which the older means of grace were still making to those Christians at Rome to whom the Epistle to the Hebrews was written? And is the writer's answer this, that the whole of the Christian life is an observance of a Day of Atonement, the eternal Day of Atonement which Christ as our High-Priest has instituted?

It is not at all impossible that this was the case, and one is the more encouraged to make the suggestion because there is the analogy of a passage in St. Paul's writings. In 1 Corinthians v. 7-8 the Apostle writes: 'Christ, our Passover-Lamb, has been sacrificed, so that we should observe our festival not with the old leaven, but with the unleavened bread of pure-mindedness and truth.' St. Paul means that the whole Christian life should be a Passover observance free from the infecting evil of tolerated sin. The writer to the Hebrews may well have had in his mind an analogous Christian use to which to put the rite of Atonement-Day.

The furniture of the Sanctuary being as has been said, the priests go constantly into the first tent in the performance of their ritual functions. Into the second tent, however, goes only the high-priest once in the year, and then never without blood, which he offers for himself and for the sins of ignorance committed by the people. Thereby the Holy Spirit makes it evident that the way into the Sanctuary was never fully disclosed so long as the first tent was standing: and this has a symbolic meaning for the present time, as showing that the gifts and sacrifices offered cannot, in the matter of conscience, perfect the worshipper (qualify him for access to God).

They are only material regulations, concerned with food and drink and various ablutions, and they apply only up to the time of the Re-ordering (ix. 6-10).

Accentuating the special character of the Day of Atonement ritual, the writer points out to his readers, (1) that only the high-priest had access to the Presence within the veil, (2) that even his approach was never unaccompanied by a sacrificial blood-offering for himself as well as for Israel, and (3) that the atonement which was effected related only to Israel's 'sins of ignorance', only to guilt and pollution unwittingly contracted. While the latter sins were real sins, involving guilt which had to be atoned for, they did not extend to cover moral offences of a deliberate nature, sins 'with respect to conscience'. As a matter of fact, in order to cover the whole area of guilt before God, Judaism had to supplement the provisions of the ritual system by piecing on to it the pardon-upon-repentance gospel preached by the prophets. The lesson which the writer to the Hebrews draws from the whole facts is the self-attested insufficiency of the old order of grace. The Holy Spirit—by which the writer here means not the principle of the new insight at work in Christianity, but the same Spirit speaking in the Old Testament through the prophets—has made it plain that, so long as the first sanctuary stood, the way into the Holy of Holies was barred, and this, says the writer pointedly, is 'a parable bearing on the present crisis'. It shows, in other words, that the gifts and sacrifices which were still being offered in Judaism had no power to qualify the worshippers in respect of conscience for access to God. Here another question of immediate critical interest comes to the front.

The insufficiency of the Jewish 'gifts and sacrifices',

says the writer, is that they are external or material ordinances, 'bearing only upon food and drink and various ablutions'. Strictly speaking, however, we cannot regard any of these regulations about food, drink, and washings as being of the substance of the sacrificial system. They belonged to it only by association, but the writer takes advantage of this association to depreciate the character of the sacrifices.

This is a point at which the main problem with which this book is concerned once again leaps to the light. Were the readers a Jewish-Christian group who, for one reason or another, were opposing the ritual freedom of the larger Church? If so, *it would be possible to find in these regulations about food and drink the real point at which, and the genuine reason for which they were holding on sentimentally to the Jewish rites and means of grace*. This in itself is not improbable, and we may compare Romans xiv. where, as has been noted, scruples with regard to food on the part of a minority in the Roman Church constitute the only error on which St. Paul takes that Church specifically to task.[1]

However that may be, these regulations cease, the writer insists, with the great 'Re-ordering' which belongs to the New Covenant, and which comes into effect with the Sacrifice made by Christ.

PRIEST THROUGH THE ETERNAL SPIRIT
(ix. 11-14)

But Christ, when He came as the High-Priest of the coming salvation, passed through the greater, more perfect tent not fashioned by hands, not part, that is, of the present creation, and taking with Him not the blood

[1] See above, p. 13.

of goats and calves but His own blood, He went in once and for all into the Holy Place, thus procuring an eternal redemption. For if the blood of goats and bulls and the ashes of a heifer sprinkled on the defiled sanctifies these persons in point of external purity, how much more shall the blood of Christ who through the Eternal Spirit offered Himself as an unblemished sacrifice to God, purify your consciences from dead works to serve the living God! (ix. 11-14).

The contrast between the atonement wrought by Christ and the old atonement is brought out by reference successively,

(a) to the heavenly shrine at which Christ's offering is presented—a shrine which is not a part or an appurtenance of this transitory world;

(b) to the character of the medium employed for the offering—the blood not of animal victims, but of Christ Himself;

(c) to the once-for-allness of Christ's entrance into the sanctuary;

(d) to the fact that the very nature of eternity is in the redemption He procures.

No explanation at all is offered why the sanctification of the worshipper, the removal of his guilt, the expiation of his sin, the atonement of his soul to God should be made dependent on the blood of sacrifice. That necessity is assumed. It is something given. It is a thing inseparable from the age-long history of grace in Israel, and the writer of this Epistle who, like a multitude of others, had found his own approach to God so prescribed and who had come along this path to the foot of the Cross, does not feel it incumbent upon him to argue its sufficiency. But while he will not enter into meta-physical questions, he will reason with us on a basis of religious experience and, within the area so indicated, he will argue from the less real to the more.

If, he argues, the ritual blood-atonement prescribed by the Jewish religion effected the 'sanctification' or cleansing of the worshipper for access to God in the matter of external purity—the writer will not claim more than this for the Jewish rites—who shall measure the effect of the blood of 'the Christ', who through 'the Eternal Spirit' offered Himself as 'an unblemished sacrifice' to God? Will it not purify the 'conscience' from dead works to serve 'a living God'? The words enclosed within inverted commas indicate the range and nature of that *plus* of grace which the writer sees provided for by the sacrifice of Jesus, and they mark the truths which he wishes to drive home upon the minds of his readers.

And what are these truths? First, the offering is the blood of the *Messiah*! The primary article of the creed of the world-mission Church was that Christ died on account of our sins (1 Corinthians xv. 3). Secondly, the offering reveals the operation of *Eternal Spirit*. The death of Jesus was no mere historical contingency but expresses the very nature of the eternal Mind and World. And because eternity is in the act, time cannot impair or devaluate its significance. Thirdly, the perfection, the *fullness* of all sacrifice is in that utter, completely moral and personal, self-devotion of Jesus to death for our sins. Fourthly, if the death of Jesus was for our sins, then, in the light of all that Jesus was and is, the atoning virtue and redemption which are in it cannot be limited in their application to ritual guilt and ignorance but extend as far as *conscience*, the moral consciousness extends: dead works, as Dr. Moffatt says, imply 'far more serious flaws and stains' than could be covered by the ritual sacrifices of the past. Fifthly, the blood of Christ brings the worshipper to *the living God*. Though this writer may not say in so many words that through Christ's action or mediation God now lives in the Christian, and the Christian in God, nothing less than this is implied in his thought of the Eternal Spirit's operation in and through the sacrifice of Jesus.

It has been pointed out by expositors that the writer to the Hebrews is silent about the love of God and the love of Christ as factors of the Atonement, and that there is nothing in his teaching about that present personal faith-union with Christ which is so vivid a part of the appropriation of grace in the Pauline theology.[1] This criticism is true, but it has been observed above [2] and will be shown more fully later, that the explanation lies essentially in the whole religious orientation of the writer's mind and particularly in the eschatological tension by which his mind is fixed continuously on the things yet to be hoped for, rather than on present conditions of inward attainment and rest. On the other hand, we should not forget those significant passages in which the author in momentary flashes lets the light in upon the present transforming reality of the Christian experience of salvation. One of these is the already discussed 'Hero-Christology' passage, ii. 14, where Christ's complete identification of Himself with us is said to have been for the purpose of overthrowing the devil's

[1] For a discriminating exposition of these and similar points see Dr. Vincent Taylor's *The Atonement in New Testament Teaching*, pp. 147-190.

[2] See pp. 52 f., 57 f., 65.

sovereignty in death, and releasing those who throughout their lives were prostrated under 'the fear of death'. Emancipation from what St. Paul calls the principalities and powers, and conquest over the last enemy were certainly a very real part of the Christian experience of grace for the man who penned these words. Even more impressive in the same connection is the present passage in which the deliverance of the conscience from the guilt and power of mortal sin is posited as a direct consequence of the atonement wrought through Jesus. For the writer of the Epistle this discharge had the reality of a fact, and it was a supreme verification of God to his spirit.

It has at the same time to be conceded that the Epistle says nothing about 'the destruction of the sinful flesh, and the satisfaction rendered to the claims of the Law', by which the Pauline interpretation of the Atonement is characterised. The argument of Hebrews, says Dr. Scott, 'has no firmer basis than the assumptions of ancient ritual'.[1] On the other hand, to depreciate these assumptions is to part company with the author of the Epistle at the nodal point of his great argument, because for him all Christianity—including all that St. Paul can read into it—is implicitly given in his formula of sanctification by the blood of Christ and in his conception of the ever-progressive access of the soul to God in Him. To regard it as a weakness in the author that, 'while he shows the inadequacy of the old ritual conceptions, he never definitely escapes from them',[2] reveals a bias in religious thinking and an application to Hebrews of categories of religious value which have their origin not in the Bible nor in New Testament Christianity but in a dualistic philosophy

[1] *The Epistle to the Hebrews*, pp. 131 f.   [2] *Ibid.*, pp. 137 f.

of the relation of matter and spirit. In this connection
no finer ultimate vindication of Hebrews from its own
standpoint could be desired than is offered by Dr.
Scott himself within the pages of his treatise.[1]

MEDIATOR OF THE NEW COVENANT
(ix. 15-22)

The writer returns again to the inseparable nexus
between the New Covenant and the redemptive sacrifice
of Christ. One sentence which he writes here is specially interesting for its close parallelism with St. Paul's
exposition of the 'Righteousness' of God in Romans
iii. 21-26. The sentence in Hebrews runs:

He is the Mediator of the New Covenant for this
reason that, now that a death has taken place for redemption from the transgressions (committed) under
the first covenant, those who are called may enter on
the eternal inheritance promised to them (ix. 15).

Both St. Paul and the writer to the Hebrews bring
the death of Christ under the rubric of 'redemption'
(*apolytrosis*), and both give this redemption a double
relation—to the past, and to the present. In Romans
the Righteousness of God which comes into operation
through the death of Christ bears (1) on the forgiveness
of sins committed in the past, (2) on the new status in
grace of the forgiven. In Hebrews, similarly, the death
of Christ (1) effects deliverance from the guilt of transgressions committed under the first covenant, (2) makes
permanent provision for the access of the elect to God
by which they are instituted into assured possession of
the promised eternal inheritance.

[1] *The Epistle to the Hebrews*, pp. 138-141.

Like St. Paul, the writer to the Hebrews takes advantage of the connection existing in the Greek language between *diatheke* in the ordinary sense of 'testamentary disposition' and *diatheke* as used in the Septuagint to render the Hebrew term *b⁰rith*, 'covenant'. In this way he establishes the formal relation between the death of Christ and the coming into force of the New Covenant. Peculiar to himself, however, is his interest in showing that under the law of Moses the 'blood of the covenant' was sprinkled on the book, the tent, and the whole paraphernalia of Hebrew worship, as well as on the people: practically everything under the Law had this ritual blood-sanctification applied to it, for 'apart from the shedding of blood', he writes, 'there is no remission of sins' (ix. 16-22).

It should be noticed that the blood-sprinkling here declared to be required by the Law extends in its range beyond the actual prescriptions for Moses' action in Exodus xxiv. 4-8, which is the basic passage on the subject. That passage, for example, does not mention the sprinkling of the book of the covenant which Moses took into his hands and read. In later usage, however, the sanctification of the book may have been included in the rite. In the commentaries attention is drawn to other slight deviations of our author from the Exodus and Leviticus texts. We may pass over these details, but shall return to the general significance of the passage presently.

Of necessity, then, since what were merely the copies of the things in heaven were purified by such means, the heavenly things themselves must be purified by better sacrifices than these. Christ has entered not a sanctuary made by hands, a mere antitype of the true, but into heaven itself, to appear now in the presence of God on our behalf: and not to offer Himself again and again, as the high-priest enters the holy place year by year, taking with him blood that is not his own. In that case, Christ would have had to suffer over and over again since the world's foundation. As it is, He has been manifested once for all, at the climax of history, to end sin by His sacrifice. And just as it is appointed for men to die once, and after that the Judgment, so also Christ, once offered in sacrifice to bear the sins of many, will appear the second time—no more to deal with sin—for the salvation of those who are awaiting Him (ix. 23-28).

The writer's conception that the things in heaven—like the book, the sanctuary, and the ritual furnishings of the Jewish worship under the Old Covenant—need to be purified by the blood of Christ surprises us at first sight, and seems to Dr. Moffatt to push the analogy of earth and heaven to fantastic lengths. But if we conceive our author to be writing to Jewish Christians who perhaps missed in the spiritual worship of Christianity the *many* holy sanctions and consecratory rites of the old religion, we shall not think it strange that he should, in effect, say to them that Christianity has its own sublime, though invisible, sanctions imparted by a greater Sacrifice. Following out this conception, we can well imagine him saying that the book of the New Covenant (the eternal gospel written in heaven, for the New Testament was not yet in being), the Christian sanctuary (the heavenly Zion, cf. xii. 18-24), and the New Israel (the Christian Church, including the company of the redeemed in heaven) have all been consecrated by the blood of Christ. The stamp of the Cross is on all of them. After all, the things in heaven represent realities which have a present existence for Christians through Christ.

The writer's point is that the sacramental element is as all-pervasive in Christianity as it is in Judaism, and its sanctions in the blood of Christ are incontestably and immeasurably greater, though they are not material. He contrasts the sacrifice of Jesus with the limited, local, impersonal, external and for ever repeated rites of the Jewish religious system (ix. 24-25). Had the Saviour's sacrifice been impersonal and merely prophetic like the latter, it would have had to be re-enacted again and again in the time-series. But just as the provisional and purely symbolic character of the Jewish rites comes out in the over-and-over-againness which cleaves as a necessity to their observance, so the perfection of the offering of Christ is expressed in the historical once-for-allness which belongs to it. It is not denied that the Saviour's Passion is eternal, but its eternity reveals itself in a single act which by the universality of its scope and the utter completeness of its intrinsic quality covers, represents, and supersedes for ever all the shadow-sacrifices which have been offered since time began.

Having said this, the writer comes to his final point. As this act of Jesus 'through the Eternal Spirit' has been effected 'at the end of the world', at the climactic moment of history, there is nothing now that can intervene between it and its sequel in the second Coming of Christ—this time not to deal with sin, since that need has been satisfied, but to complete the salvation of those who await Him.

The return of the writer to his eschatology in the words 'He will appear the second time', etc. (ix. 28), shows that *his great elaboration of the Alexandrian*

*contrast of earthly and heavenly reality has been but
an interlude in the development of his central theme.*
The apocalyptic distinction of the Two Ages of time,
though crossed by the idealistic antithesis of the Two
Worlds of reality, has not been absorbed into or lost in
the latter. The original current of the writer's thought
resumes its strong flow the moment it has passed
through the broad reaches of the Alexandrian section
in chapters viii.-ix. Nor does he, like the Fourth
Evangelist, resolve the Parousia into terms which
include or involve the eternal mystical presence of the
Saviour with His Church. He does not break with the
apocalyptic hope even in an unconscious way. The
eternal world, in breaking into time in the Incarnation
of the Saviour, does not cease to be the eternal world.
The curve of its intersection with the world of time is—
to use a mathematical illustration—like the parabola
or hyperbola which, coming from infinity, recedes
again into infinity. One focus, represented by the
Incarnation and Atonement-sacrifice of Jesus, has
appeared in time. The other, represented by the
Second Advent, lies wholly beyond. But the writer's
eyes are fixed in its direction. 'He will appear the
second time—no more to deal with sin—for the salvation
of those who await Him.' 'In ever so short a time now
the Coming One will arrive, He will linger no more'
(x. 37). That the writer can relate eternity and time
in the way he does gives us the measure of his faith,
but he does so relate them.

Before returning to his eschatology in the last
chapters of the book, the writer will gather up the
various aspects of Christ into one supreme presentation.

THE OFFERING OF THE BODY OF CHRIST
(x. 1-18)

We are reminded that the repetition year by year of the same sacrifices in Judaism cannot perfect the approach of the worshippers to God, and that for a definite reason.

The Law has in it only a shadow of the future order of salvation. It does not present the actual image of the facts. . . . For in that case would not the sacrifices have ceased to be offered, since the worshippers once purified would no longer retain any consciousness of sins? On the contrary, what the sacrifices bring with them, year by year, is the remembrance of our sins, for it is an impossible thing for the blood of bulls and goats to take our sins away (x. 1-4).

It is interesting that the writer here, taking his stand now on the facts of experience, limits the efficacy of the Jewish rites to the negative function of bringing home to the conscience the fact and the guilt of sin. Because this consciousness is for ever renewed at the altar, it is impossible for the sacrifices to 'take away' our sins. With this declaration of the 'impossibility' attaching to the cultus we may compare St. Paul's analogous affirmation of the disability cleaving to the Law as a system of moral demand (Romans viii. 3). St. Paul is indicting the failure of the Law to conquer the power of sin in our nature, the writer to the Hebrews is impeaching the cultus for its failure to remove the sense of the uncleanness of our souls before God. Both theologians are writing from the standpoint of a higher revelation than Judaism had received, as the writer to the Hebrews will presently make perfectly clear.

Meantime, let there be no undervaluing of the real, though negative, function assigned to the cultus in bringing home to the soul the 'remembrance' of sin. The sacrificial worship kept alive the sense of the Holiness of God and, like the Law in the Pauline theology, it prepared the way for the higher revelation of grace in the gospel. If anyone should doubt this, let him read Isaiah's account of the fundamental experience which made him a prophet. It was in the Temple, amid the elevated associations of the place and the worship, that the transforming vision of the Lord 'high and lifted up' appeared to Isaiah, and it was with fire from off the altar that his consecration came (Isaiah vi. 1-5).

Hence, when He comes into the world, it is with the word: 'Thou hast not willed sacrifice and offering, but Thou hast prepared a body for Me; Thou hast not approved whole-burnt offerings and sin-offerings. Thereupon I said, See, I come—it is so written in the roll of the book concerning Me—to do Thy will, O God' (x. 5-7).

It is by a daring thought that the writer takes the prophetic passage, Psalm xl. 6-8, and gives it a direct relation to the Incarnation of the Saviour. He is not citing the psalmist's words as an interesting illustration or anticipation of the spirit in which the Redeemer acted, but as a factual prediction of the Incarnation by the pre-existent Son of God speaking overhead of the psalmist. The words are quoted from the Septuagint version which, in place of the 'My ears Thou hast opened' of the Hebrew text of the sixth verse of the Psalm, has the reading 'Thou hast prepared a body for Me'. According to this rendering the Christ of the Psalm is not rejecting sacrifice and offering in favour of something else, but rejecting animal sacrifice in favour of that personal sacrifice which God has willed from Him, and for which He has prepared by appointing for Him the body of His Incarnation.

Here then, according to the writer, is the *modus operandi* of the divine grace in Christianity. *It does not abolish the principle of sacrifice, but by its own consummate provision it abolishes the guilt of sin.* Under the Jewish cultus this guilt of sin was only confirmed and renewed by the sacrifices. Now it is 'taken away'. In the divine Will, accepted by the Christ of God, there is made possible, through the complete personal and spiritual self-identification of the Christ with men, that *actual* assumption of human guilt which was only formally represented in the Jewish rites. For this theologian the taking of our guilt upon Himself by the Redeemer in the body of His Incarnation is so real and absolute a fact for faith that there comes with it a clearance of conscience and a sense of atonement with God such as under the first covenant, though signified in shadow, remained actually unachieved.

The passage brings out very clearly the continuity of the pre-existent life of Jesus with His Incarnate life, and the continuity in turn of the Incarnation with His heavenly life. He assumed manhood to fulfil a purpose declared in eternity, offering Himself to God 'through the eternal Spirit', and now in eternity He presents the result of that finished work. It may be through this strong insistence on the continuity of the Christ-manifestation that, as Dr. E. F. Scott points out, the Resurrection of Christ as a separate moment in the manifestation has not the place or critical significance

K

in Hebrews which it possesses in the Christology of the New Testament in general.[1]

He clears away the first (order) in order to establish the second. And it is by this will of His that we have been consecrated—through the offering, once for all, of the Body of Jesus Christ. . . . He by the offering of one sacrifice for sins has seated Himself ' for ever ' at the right hand of God, to await the time when His enemies are made a footstool for His feet. By one offering He has perfected the sanctified for ever (x. 9-10, 12-14).

So, after his rich development of the conception of Christ's oblation, the writer focusses the minds of his readers on the eschatological end of God's purpose in Christ. But before concluding the section, and in order to bring out the reality of the status of the Christian in grace, he reverts to the promise which forms the climax of Jeremiah's prediction of the New Covenant of God.

Putting My laws in their hearts, I will inscribe them also on their minds. And their sins and their transgressions I will never remember again (x. 16-17).

We see here that the writer's Christianity is not entirely that of a futurist hope, however enthralling and engrossing, but starts from an experience of actualised grace which has already in it the essence of what the forward-looking religion of the past descried only in vision.

And where there is this forgiveness, offering for sin no longer has any place (x. 18).

It is surely relevant to observe that, if the writer of the Epistle was merely seeking to establish the grandeur,

[1] *The Epistle to the Hebrews*, pp. 153 f.

the finality, the absoluteness of Christianity compared with other religions, as the exponents of the modern interpretation of Hebrews assert, he could have dispensed with the so-often repeated reminder to his readers that the order, the rites and the sacrifices of Judaism were *ended*. It would have been enough to show that Christianity transcended Judaism, the noblest religion of the past, without insisting *pari passu* and all the time that it abrogated and superseded it. But the latter insistence would be of the very essence of the matter if he were writing to Jewish Christians on whom the hand of the past still lay very heavily.

It remains to consider two sections of the Epistle which bear on the same thematic subject.

THE NEW CHRISTIAN APPROACH TO GOD
(xii. 18-24)

It is not to a tangible world that you have drawn near, a blaze of fire, a mist, a gloom, a tempest, a trumpet blast, a voice speaking things such that those who heard them prayed that not another word should be added; for they could not endure the injunction that 'If even a beast touch the mountain, it shall be stoned'. So dreadful indeed was the manifestation that Moses said, ' I am terrified and shudder'. No! You have come to Mount Zion, to the city of the living God, the heavenly Jerusalem, to the myriads of angels, to the assembly and Church of the first-born whose names are enrolled in heaven, to the God of all as judge, to the spirits of the just made perfect, to Jesus the mediator of the new covenant, and to the sprinkled blood which speaks a better message than Abel (xii. 18-24).

Access to God, the admission of the purified soul to the divine Presence, remains for the writer to the

Hebrews the dominant and final norm of the Christian life.[1] But this approach is circumstanced by the character of the world revealed to the worshipper in the Christian theophany, and here the writer in magnificent words contrasts the numinous environment of Israel at Mount Sinai with the greater glory that opens on Christian eyes in the approach to the heavenly Zion, the city of the God of life. Both environments are numinous; both are charged with the presence of the *mysterium tremendum* which is God; but they are not *in pari materia*. It is not to a new Sinai with a repetition of its storm-phenomena that the Christian now goes forward, nor to the dread commandments of a new prohibitory Law—for the numinous element at Sinai was not constituted by signs and portents alone but by the words of terror spoken in the decalogue and in the regulations for the cultus. The Christian approach is circumstanced by grace, grace expressed in the city of God and in the myriads of worshipping angels—ministering spirits all of them—who in festal assembly with the redeemed, the spirits of the just now at last in perfect fellowship with God, constitute the holy, supernatural environment of the Church on earth. Above all, the approach is to Jesus, the Mediator of the New Covenant, and to a sprinkled blood which speaks more eloquently and in more blessed terms than Abel (cf. xi. 4). For while Abel's blood cries from the ground for vengeance, denouncing Cain and excluding him from God, the blood of Jesus invites the sinner's repentance and return. The writer does not forget that the God of all is still the judge of all, and that the voice which once shook the earth is soon to shake both heaven and earth (xii. 26), but between the sinner

[1] See above, pp. 66 f.

and the holy God there has stepped the Mediator of the New Covenant, the great atoning High-Priest of our confession, our Advocate with God.

The writer to the Hebrews, then, will remind his readers that it is not a case—as perhaps in their contemporary mood they sadly thought—of Jerusalem being no more, of the angels of the Law and the holy prerogatives of Israel, the firstborn of God, being ignored, of the covenant with God being rescinded and the sacramental cultus and all its sanctions being abandoned. In the new approach to God through Jesus the people of Jesus will find all these things again, not indeed in the old form in which they were at best only shadow-shapes or simulacra of the things in heaven, but sublimated, spiritualised, eternalised, and perfected. But let the readers beware that they do not at this last critical hour turn away from Him who, greater than Moses, now speaks to them from *heaven*!

THE CHRISTIAN ALTAR
(xiii. 10-14)

We have an altar which confers no authorisation to eat from it on those who minister (or worship) in the tent. For the bodies of those animals, whose blood is brought by the high-priest into the sanctuary 'as an offering for sin', are consumed by fire 'outside the camp'. For this reason Jesus also, to sanctify the people by His own blood, suffered outside the gate. Therefore let us go out to Him, outside the camp, bearing the shame He bore, for we have no permanent city here, but seek the one to come (xiii. 10-14).

The Christian group at Rome to which our author

writes was, by his own showing (xiii. 9), in danger of being 'led astray' or swept from the course by doctrines of a kind alien to Christianity, which turned apparently on 'foods'. His reply is that it is a right thing to have the 'heart', that is the mind or will, fortified or re-assured, but this can only come by 'grace'. It will not come by the observance of food-laws which have never in the past helped those who submitted themselves to their discipline. There can be little doubt here that the writer's allusion is to Jewish regulations which were being commended at Rome as an aid to faith, and that the propaganda owed the strength of its appeal, in the last resort, to the association of these ritual regulations with the cultus of the past. It was from this cultus, from the altar of Judaism, that the sanctions for the ordinances were derived.[1] Was there to be no altar in the religion of the Messiah as the source of holy aids to living?

The writer's reply is that there is an altar in Christianity, but it is of a very different character from the altar as conceived in these Judaising doctrines. No analogy of any kind exists between the Oblation of Christ and those Jewish sacrifices from which food was carried away for the use of the ministrants or worshippers at the shrine. The only analogy which the offering of Christ has with the sacrifices of the past is limited to the whole-burnt 'offering for sin' in which, after the blood of the victims was carried by the high-priest into the Holy of Holies, their bodies were totally consumed by fire outside the camp of Israel. So it was that Jesus made His self-offering. He who came to sanctify Israel by His blood suffered death 'outside the gate'. What, then, is the Christian altar? Is it

[1] See above, pp. 132 f.

Golgotha? It lies certainly beyond the bounds of the terrestrial Jerusalem, and it is the altar of the Saviour's martyrdom. We must therefore 'go out' to Jesus, to where He was crucified 'outside the camp', and must take our share of the shame He bore. This last appeal indicates with sufficient clearness the nature of the influences which were retarding the group from the open profession of Christianity and inclining it to draw in various ways within the protection of the *religio licita* of Judaism. And here the writer is given a supreme chance to assert once again the eschatological character of the Christian calling.

> 'Let us go out to Him, outside the camp . . . for we have here no permanent city, but we seek the one to come.'

This going out—the putting into practice of the great watch-word of Stephen and of the world-mission—is the true Christian approach to the altar; the sharing of the reproach of Christ is the true Christian communion of the altar; and it is in this going out and in this communion that the 'grace' is to be experienced, by which, and not by archaistic observance of food-regulations, the spirit is to be fortified.

Much has been written on this difficult passage by exegetes of different schools in the effort to discover its relation to the Christian Eucharist.[1] There are those who, unable to find themselves in the thought that the writer could at this point omit all reference to the communion of the Body and Blood of Christ, have by

[1] On the whole question see, besides the *Commentaries* of Westcott and Moffatt, Dr. Vincent Taylor's *The Atonement in New Testament Teaching*, pp. 153-161.

dexterities of exegesis identified the altar with the table of the Lord. On this view we might interpret the passage thus: 'We Christians have our altar, but it is not one at which those who minister or worship in the (Jewish) tabernacle have authority to eat.' In other words, we Christians have our sacramental food, but this food has nothing whatsoever to do with the ritual food-laws of Judaism. So Bishop Westcott in his *Commentary*: he understands the writer to mean that 'our great sin-offering, consumed in one sense outside the gate, is given to us as our food. The Christian, therefore, who can partake of Christ offered for his sins, is admitted to a privilege unknown under the Old Covenant'. But this understanding, which in any case reads more into the text than is really there, fails altogether to do justice to the thought of the *holocaust* sacrifice which the writer declares to be the only admissible analogy to the offering of Jesus to be found in the Jewish cultus. For at the holocaust altar nothing of any kind was eaten. It can hardly be maintained then that the writer has in his mind at this point the relation of Christ's sacrifice to the sacrament of the Holy Communion. But it is equally gratuitous, and just as tendentious, to fasten attention on the writer's words here and on his omission at an earlier point to make any reference to the 'bread and wine' offering which Melchizedek brought to Abraham, and to take these as evidences of a declared disapproval of some supposed materialistic interpretation of the sacrament in some quarter of the contemporary Hellenistic Church, as if the writer were purposely denying all connection between the death of Christ outside the gate and that communion with the Lord which St. Paul describes in 1 Corinthians x. 16-22 and xi. 23-29. So Dr. Peake in the Century Bible volume on Hebrews, and so Dr. Moffatt in his *Commentary*. In actual fact the passage gives us no positive indication that the writer has the Christian sacrament of communion in mind in this context.

But if nothing is said in Hebrews about the Lord's Supper, is that any stranger than the total omission of all reference to the same sacrament in St. Paul's Epistle to the Romans? In the case of Hebrews the special explanation exists that the writer is so swept onwards throughout the whole Epistle by the tide of his eschatological passion that he is carried past all intermediate stages of communion with the Lord on the way.[1] The absence of the Holy Supper from his itinerary of the way goes with the omission of all that mysticism of present faith-union with Christ which lies so near to the heart of St. Paul. He writes to brace his readers for the eschatological journey which is for him the very essence of the Christian calling. We have here no continuing city. We have not even resting-places by the way. Even St. Paul, who rejoices that life to him is Christ, can, when speaking of himself as a prisoner at Rome undergoing trials not very different from those of some of the Roman Christians to whom Hebrews is addressed, confess himself inwardly divided and embarrassed: 'I long', he writes (Philippians i. 23), 'to depart and to be with Christ, for that is very much better.'

It remains, however, that between the writer to the Hebrews and St. Paul there is a wide difference in the manner in which the central mystery of the Christian religion, the Atonement wrought by Christ, is ap-

[1] See also above, p. 136, and the Note which concludes the present section.

proached. With St. Paul it is instinctive to relate the
event on Calvary immediately to the inward and
personal experience of the Christian. It is not enough
to contemplate the drama of redemption in its cosmic
and objective character: to receive and believe that
Christ entered into history, lived as man, suffered in
the flesh, died on the Cross, revealed God's righteousness with relation to sin, was raised from the dead by
the glory of the Father and was exalted to the right
hand of God. All this must have its reflex for St. Paul
in the inner domain of the Christian spirit. Christ
lives in the Christian (Galatians ii. 20), is incarnated or
'formed' in the Christian (Galatians iv. 20). As Christ
died, so the Christian dies to sin, and as Christ was
raised from the dead by the glory of the Father, so the
Christian rises to a resurrection life (Romans vi. 1-14).
So also he ascends with the exalted Christ, and is glorified with Him in the heavenly places (Colossians iii. 1-3).
All acts and episodes in the cosmic manifestation of
Christ have their instant counterpart in the human
experience of redemption. On the other hand, in the
writer to the Hebrews there is not this point-with-point
correspondence.

For the writer to the Hebrews salvation depends
indeed, and depends absolutely, on the act of Christ's
supreme sacrifice. But it is not considered 'how that
self-offering becomes a vital reality in the experience
of believers'.[1] There is no reference to justification, to
reconciliation, to peace with God, to the death or
destruction of sin in the flesh, or to resurrection to newness of life as present and inward realities. But this
is primarily because in Hebrews the eyes are on Christ
and on the consummation of His work in *heaven*. The

[1] Vincent Taylor, *op. cit.*, pp. 161 f.

whole response of the Christian soul to God is com-
prehended in the soul's absorption in its heavenly
calling (xii. 1-2). For the writer the whole revelation
of God in Christ and all the blessings of grace are
centred in the Priesthood of Christ and in the effects
of His priestly work as we draw near to God through
Him. But it is made quite clear that in this approach
to God we experience much. We experience absolution
from guilt (i. 3, etc.), the expiation of our sins (ii. 17,
etc.), the cleansing of our consciences (ix. 14), the
'sanctification' of our persons (x. 10), the removal of
the barriers between our souls and God (x. 19-23) and
the impartation of the Holy Spirit and the powers of
the World to Come (vi. 4-5). By His one offering Christ,
says the writer, 'has perfected the sanctified for ever';
He has put them, that is, into unhindered communion
with God.

NOTE.—The difficulty of bringing the sacrament of
the Holy Communion in the Church into relation with
the writer's insistence on the holocaust nature of the
Saviour's oblation is not insuperable. While the
problem is not to be solved either by exegetics of the
type of Dr. Westcott's or by critical negations of the
type of Dr. Peake's or Dr. Moffatt's, it does admit of
possible solution along other lines of approach. At
the institution of the Supper the Body and Blood of
Christ were present in His living person and as such
they were sacramentally offered. The Body was that
which *was to be* broken on the Cross. The Blood was
that which *was to be* shed. In this sense all of the terms
used of the elements in the accounts of Mark, Paul,
Matthew, and Luke admit of being understood. Jesus
was associating His followers with His *impending*

sacrifice, and was thus consecrating them for the Kingdom of God. In receiving the bread and the cup these followers were sacramentally receiving the Lord's Body and Blood as devoted by Him *beforehand* to death. What they hereafter commemorate before God is the supreme self-oblation of the *living* Lord. The altar from which the gifts are given is the Upper Room, not Golgotha, which was not yet present except in anticipation. In this way it can be held that the strictures of the writer to the Hebrews, his insistence on the difference between the sacrifice offered by Christ and the ordinary sacrifices offered on Jewish altars, do not exclude the reality of the meaning which the Church attaches to the observance of the Eucharist service.

Conclusions from Chapters IV and V

The evidence furnished by the theological material of the Epistle to the Hebrews agrees very closely in form and substance with the conclusions drawn from the admonitory sections as summarised at the end of Chapter III.

I. The emphasis of the writer on the supernal and heavenly character of the Christian revelation and on the transcendence of the Person and Work of Christ over the Old Testament religion of the Law and the Cultus is strongly and evenly maintained from the first page of the Epistle (i. 2) to the last (xiii. 13-14). The Alexandrianism of the middle section of the Epistle (vii.-x.) is but an interlude designed to explicate and enforce the central eschatological appeal.

II. The Epistle is directed to a minority group in the Church which is failing to grasp the significance of the Church's faith in the heavenly Priesthood and Oblation of Christ, and is intended to promote their fuller understanding of this mystery. But there is nothing which *explicitly* designates the group as Jewish-Christian or otherwise.

III. On the other hand, the consistent theological teaching of the Epistle is *compatible* with the hypothesis that the persons addressed were Jewish-Christian in origin, background, and sympathy. And throughout the work (*a*) the author's selection of topics for didactic exposition, (*b*) the form and direction of his argument, and (*c*) the character of his particular emphases, all gain in intelligibility and point if we suppose the group to be conservatively Jewish-Christian in sentiment and tendency. The like does not at all hold true if we assume for the group a Gentile-Christian background.

Thus in a passage of pivotal importance (ii. 10-18),[1] where the writer had before him *other* possibilities of developing his great Christological theme, it is remarkable that he turns at once and irreversibly for all the rest of the Epistle to what can only be described as a hieratical and ritual interpretation of Christ as our High-Priest after the order of Melchizedek. Why does he base his whole Christological argument from the Old Testament on the fulfilment of the priesthood and the cultus in Jesus? And why, in another passage (vii. 11-19),[2] and yet another (x. 9-10),[3] is he so emphatic in his insistence that in Christ the Levitical priesthood, the ordinances, and the sacrifices have been not only transcended but *abolished*?

So again why does he, in speaking of the inability of the gifts and sacrifices offered in Judaism to qualify

[1] See above, pp. 101-105.   [2] Above, pp. 114-116.
[3] Above, pp. 146-147.

the worshipper in the matter of conscience for approach to God (ix. 6-10),[1] say so surprising a thing as that these gifts and sacrifices were only material regulations concerned with food and drink, etc. ? The only plausible explanation is that doctrines of a Jewish kind regarding food and drink constituted a danger to the community (xiii. 9),[2] and were being propagated on the ground of their sanction in the Jewish cultus.

Similar questions are raised for us, as we have seen, by the predilection of the writer for details like the furnishings of the tabernacle (ix. 1-5),[3] his emphasis on the purification of the things in heaven (ix. 23-28),[4] his sublimation of the ancient sanctities in his glowing picture of the glories of the heavenly world (xii. 18-24),[5] and his delineation of the Christian life as a going forth to Jesus 'without the camp' (xiii. 10-14).[6] All of these features, as we have seen, acquire a real explanation and point the moment it is assumed that the group had sentimental leanings towards the old religion of Judaism with its worship, sanctions, sacraments, holy prerogatives and means of grace. None of them has equal point and intelligibility if we place the group against an Ethnic-Christian background.

IV. Once again, we have found no trace of the Gnostic or pagan aberrations to which Gentile Christians would be ordinarily exposed.

[1] See above, pp. 132-133.
[2] Above, pp. 149-150.
[3] Above, pp. 130 f.
[4] Above, pp. 140 f.
[5] Above, pp. 147-149.
[6] Above, pp. 149-151.

CHAPTER VI

THE PLACE OF THE EPISTLE IN EARLY CHRISTIAN HISTORY AND IN THE NEW TESTAMENT

THE MINORITY GROUP AT ROME

IN Chapter I of the present work, after some preliminary survey of earlier and more recent approaches to an understanding of the Epistle to the Hebrews, the opinion was expressed that neither of the two main critical theories dividing the field at the present time could be considered satisfactory in an historical point of view. Neither theory had brought the situation reflected in the Epistle into exact and adequate focus, and neither, therefore, could be thought to have done full justice to its character and purport. It was contended, accordingly, that a place existed for a new approach to the Epistle based on a reconsideration of its historical setting. Questions of an important kind had come to the surface in the course of the discussion, and at the end of the first chapter an outline sketch was given of positions towards which the present writer felt himself pointed by his personal study of the evidence. The first of these was that the key to Hebrews, alike in its practical and in its theoretical aspects, was to be found only by bringing the Epistle into close integration with historical and doctrinal developments occurring within the sphere of the world-mission of Christianity as inaugurated by Stephen and his successors.

In Chapter II, accordingly, an inquiry into the Stephen records in Acts vi.-vii. was undertaken, and the points of contact between the teaching of the protomartyr and the theology of Hebrews were found to be so numerous and substantial as to suggest the strong probability of some organic relationship between the two. Stephen's stress on the transcendent and heavenly end of the Christian calling and his doctrine of the supersession of the Jewish cultus by Jesus were noted as primary points of agreement between Stephen and the Epistle, and the possibility of such doctrine creating divisions of sympathy within Jewish-Christian circles in the world-mission Church was taken into consideration.[1] At the end of Chapter II the way seemed open to go forward to the Epistle with the presumption in our minds that the teaching of Stephen might not only prove to have been the matrix in which the main theological ideas elaborated in Hebrews were formed, but might also explain the rise within the Church at Rome of a minority group reacting against the larger freedom of world-mission Christianity. Such a minority would presumably put forward principles and claims of its own counter to those of the world-Church and not very different in their tendency from those of the 'Hebrew' section of the Mother Church at Jerusalem.

The writer to the Hebrews would, on this view, be an ardent adherent to the principles of Stephen and the world-mission, who employed his special Jewish-Hellenist theological and dialectical equipment to bring this disaffected minority to a better mind. The members of the group were personally known to him, and he believed them to be drifting in a direction inimical and indeed disastrous to their continued

[1] See above, pp. 42-44.

Christian existence. In Chapter II all this was put forward simply as an hypothesis which needed to be tested by detailed study of the evidence of the Epistle, and the examination of this evidence has engaged us throughout the greater part of Chapters III-V.

The results of the inquiry in Chapters III-V have been re-assuring. The futurist outlook and the Christological emphases of the Epistle to the Hebrews have been found to be in the direct line of Stephen's teaching. While the 'Hebrew' character of the group addressed nowhere comes to surface statement in the letter—for the writer never once makes any use of the terms Jew, Gentile, Hebrew, or Greek—the evidence of the Epistle from first to last has been found to be compatible with the hypothesis of the Jewish-Christian extraction and background of the group and with its 'Hebrew' tendencies. Not only so, but the form, the matter, and the emphases of the writer's argument have been seen to acquire new force, relevance, and illumination the moment the hypothesis is assumed to represent the truth of the situation, while no such result follows upon the adoption of any rival theory.

Attention has been called, moreover, to the conspicuous absence from the Epistle of all traces of pagan Hellenistic ideas affecting the mind of the community. In the light of all this, the initial presumption with which the inquiry started has developed a probability-value far exceeding that of a mere provisional hypothesis, and we seem justified in concluding that the Jewish-Christian character of the group has been proved, proved, that is, as far as any conclusion of the kind can be established by inductive reasoning.

At the same time evidence has been adduced in the same chapters which amounts to a fair demonstration

L

of the second, third, and fifth of the theses provisionally stated at the end of Chapter I.

It now becomes possible, therefore, to resume the thread of the argument broken off at the end of Chapter II, where the question concerned the complexion of the 'Hebrew' minority forming a section of the Jewish-Hellenist Church at Rome. We shall investigate later the important evidence furnished by St. Paul's Epistle to the Romans with regard to that Church as a whole and with regard to its divisions. Meantime attention needs to be focussed on a passage which has not yet been examined, but which now confronts us squarely, coming as it does in sequence to the impressive statement of what constitutes the Christian life from the standpoint of the writer to the Hebrews (xii. 1-3).

Resistance unto Blood.—The Question of the Date of Hebrews

You have not yet resisted to the death in the conflict with sin (xii. 4).

This passage, like vi. 9-10 and x. 32-34, lets the light in upon the history and the situation of the Christians addressed in the letter. But while those earlier passages allude to past achievements of Christian fidelity and fortitude which the writer recalls as an incentive to the community to regain confidence in its calling under the existing conditions, this later statement refers to an experience which has not yet been encountered but which may well be part of the prospect now confronting the group.

It is true that the author nowhere else speaks of martyrdom as a concomitant or inevitable issue of the

Christian calling, nor is it certain that the present statement means anything more than that the Christians addressed have not yet as a matter of fact answered for their faith with their lives, as so many of the faithful who now form the great cloud of witnesses have had to do.   Dr. Moffatt therefore deprecates the reading into the writer's words of any necessary or ideal sequence of martyrdom upon a convinced faith.   But even if it should be granted that the sequence in question had not the character of an ideal necessity for the mind of the rigorist theologian who wrote the Epistle to the Hebrews, account has to be taken of historical *circumstances* as a possible determinative factor in the case.

The supreme interest of the passage does, indeed, lie in the question of its historical bearings at this point. What was the nature of the situation which the writer contemplates? He has in a previous passage reminded his readers of 'the former days' of suffering through which they passed after their first conversion to the faith, when they were publicly exposed to contumely and insult (x. 32-34). This—if our interpretation of the event has been correct [1]—was in A.D. 49, the year of the Claudian edict imposing extradition on the Jews of Rome. Though confiscations of property and imprisonments had occurred in the pogrom at that time, there had been no loss of Christian lives. Now circumstances exist under which, if the writer's words do not merely chronicle a past fact, death for the faith will have to be reckoned with as a real contingency of the Christian calling. When, then, were the words written? On the understanding of the earlier time of troubles just referred to, we should have to suppose a date sufficiently ahead of A.D. 49 to enable that year to be

[1] See above, pp. 40-41, 71 f.

recalled as 'the former days', yet not so late as the time
of the Neronian persecution when red martyrdom came
to the Church. We should then have to assume that
in the interval since A.D. 49 conditions had changed for
the worse, so far as the Christians at Rome were concerned. The tide of public disfavour and suspicion
was now running against Christians rather than
against Jews. Ideas were abroad in certain quarters
which, later on, were to lend colour to Nero's infamous
charge against the confessors of Christ, and among
some of the latter the temptation may have been
present to draw themselves more closely under the
shelter of the permitted religion of Judaism. If this
should be accepted as a credible account of the situation
of the minority group to which Hebrews was written,
it would enable us to place the date of the Epistle at
some point *before* the Neronian persecution, say about
the end of the sixth Christian decade or the beginning
of the seventh. This would be a year or two after St.
Paul wrote his Epistle to the Romans, roughly, therefore, around A.D. 60.

But there is another interpretation which might
conceivably be placed on the words, 'You have not yet
resisted unto blood'—the Greek verb used is an aorist
—and this has to be considered before any final decision
on the question of the date of the Epistle can be taken.
On this interpretation, the situation would be *later* than
the Neronian persecution, and the meaning of the
passage would be that the Christian group addressed,
unlike other Christians at Rome, escaped the blood-
bath of that killing-time. We might then suppose the
explanation of their escape to have been that they had
for various reasons assumed the protective colouring
of the Jewish religion and its rites. A group of Jewish

Christians still continuing to live within the synagogue had presented to the world only the Jewish side of its confession, and so avoided exposure to the charge of complicity in the crime of Christianity: this not by intention or calculation possibly, but none the less really. With the impulse to seek the protective coloration of the Jewish religion would go naturally that strong sentiment towards the Old Testament provisions for ritual holiness in drawing near to God which, to judge by the evidence of various passages of the Epistle, was characteristic of these Christians and comes to expression particularly in the attraction exercised over them by Jewish food-regulations of one sort or another (ix. 10, xiii. 9).[1] If this could be presumed a possible interpretation of the actual situation, it would be open to us to date the Epistle at some point *after* the storm fell on the Church under Nero.

Grave objections present themselves, however, against the putting of this construction on the writer's words. Had the group addressed been guilty of such dissembling under the colour of the Jewish religion, it is inconceivable that fuller notice would not have been taken of it by the writer. We should have expected the infamy to resound through every page of his letter, nor would it be easy to explain the courteous and unconstrained friendliness of his general tone towards the readers. Apart from this it is not certain that adhesion to synagogue forms and rites would have procured for these Christians complete protection from delation by Jewish or other informers. For these reasons it is difficult to think that the passage can relate to the period after Nero unless we place the time so much later that the generation addressed was not in

[1] Above, pp. 132-133, 149-150.

existence at the time of the Neronian persecution or
was not sufficiently adult to experience the full brunt
of that event. In that case, what becomes of the former
ordeal through which the Christians addressed had
actually had to pass in terms of x. 32-34? That ordeal
cannot on this hypothesis be connected either with the
happenings in A.D. 49 or with the Neronian attack on
the Church, but must relate to some later time of
trouble about which we know nothing. But while the
possibility of such a late date cannot absolutely be
excluded, there is nothing in the internal character of
the situation implied in the letter or in its theology
definitely to demand it. On the contrary, the strength
of the sentiment which—if our interpretation of the
Epistle as a whole is correct—impelled the Jewish-
Christian minority group at Rome towards an interest
in the cultic provisions of Judaism is more intelligible
if the altar and the sacrificial worship of Judaism were
still in existence, in other words, if the situation was
prior to A.D. 70. While therefore absolute proof of the
date of Hebrews is not forthcoming from the evidence
furnished by the letter, the balance of probability
inclines on the whole in favour of the pre-Neronian
theory, against which, in any case, there lies no insuperable objection. It is not necessary on other grounds to
assume a Domitianic date. The choice of a year round
A.D. 60 will reasonably satisfy all the requirements of
the case, and has the advantage of leaving room for
the possibility that in his strong accentuation in chapter
iii. of the 'forty years' period of the divine probation
of Israel after the Exodus the writer has his mind on
the chronology of the contemporary Christian situation.
A forty years' period of Christianity, calculated from
the advent of salvation in 'the word spoken by the

Lord' (ii. 3), would be running towards its close at the time the Epistle was written, but had not yet expired. The dating of the work about A.D. 60, when Christianity had entered on its fourth decade, would be consonant enough with the general evidence of the Epistle.

THE WRITER OF THE EPISTLE

It would agree with the evidence of Hebrews as a whole if we conceived the writer to be an Alexandrian Jew who had received his institution in Christianity from followers of Stephen. These would be men who had 'heard', not necessarily the Lord Himself, though that is the meaning ordinarily put upon ii. 3, but the word of salvation originally delivered in the teaching of Jesus, and whose witness to that word at Alexandria, Rome, and elsewhere had been attested by the same kind of numinous signs and wonders as had attested Stephen (ii. 4; cf. Acts vi. 8-10). The writer's principles from the start would be the principles of the proto-martyr, who saw that in Jesus the Age of the End had declared itself, and *Finis* had been written to the Law and the ordinances of the past. St. Paul had shown Christ to be the End of the Law. The writer to the Hebrews, travelling along a different but parallel line, concentrates on the Cultus, and provides the necessary supplement to St. Paul. He will show that in the Oblation of Jesus the divine eternal purpose for the sacrificial cleansing of the guilt of man had attained its perfect consummation. It was as plain to this man from the 110th Psalm that Jesus was the High-Priest of our salvation as that He was the Lord enthroned at the right hand of God with all His adversaries under His feet. He, like Stephen, knew that in Jesus something 'greater than the Temple' had appeared, and that an Atonement for sins had been offered beside which 'the blood of beasts on Jewish altars' was but a shadow or prefigurement. To develop the full pregnancy of Stephen's insistence on the supra-historical goal of the Christian calling he summoned to his aid all the resources of the Jewish-Alexandrian Wisdom theology with its Platonic distinction of the phenomenal and the real and its counterpointing of earthly and heavenly existence; but he did so only in the service of his world-renouncing religion, not for its philosophical or theological interest.

The group of self-isolated Jewish Christians at Rome to whom he wrote the Epistle were, for reasons intelligibly enough connected with the duress of their position, tempted to accentuate one-sidedly the Jewish element in their inheritance, and were living so entirely on the sub-Christian level of their religion, that to him, with his uncompromising insistence on the world-renouncing character of Christianity, they seemed to be turning from Christ and forfeiting their share in the World to Come.

To avert this catastrophe, this atrophy of Christian existence, this loss of hold on God's calling, this forfeiture of eternal life, the writer develops an argument which in its range and magnificence of religious and theological insight soars perhaps far above what the immediate exigencies of the particular situation demanded. Yet not as one developing a gnosis or carrying Christian doctrine to new or speculative conclusions. The structure of doctrine which he builds up is rooted in the actualities of the human need before him, and its principles are the basic principles of the Church's *homologia* or confession. But just because he develops these articles of belief to the full height of their significance the Epistle is a document of supreme and universal interest.

Whereas Stephen had preached that Jesus had transcended and superseded the cultus and the law of Judaism, this writer will show that He did so by His complete, vicarious, sacrificial identification of Himself with humanity. And it is the measure of the hierophantic insight and power which he brought to the execution of his task that, while moving among ancient symbols and concepts, Hebrew and Greek, he yet by the intense realism of his presentation of the Incarnation appeals more intimately to certain of the profoundest sensibilities of our modern age than any other writer in the New Testament.

Who was the writer? We shall not expect to be wiser in this matter than the ancient Church and Origen. From the reference in xiii. 24 to 'our brother Timothy' it is naturally to be inferred that the writer stood in some relationship to the Pauline world-mission circle, and the tradition of the Pauline authorship of Hebrews, which came to Alexandria with the Epistle, may have had no other basis than that passage. But the Pauline authorship, though it was so strongly entrenched in Alexandrian belief as to command the deference of Origen, was felt to conflict so greatly with the language and style of St. Paul that Origen, as we saw, gave out that only the matter was of Paul; the book itself was a *scholion* on St. Paul's ideas drawn up by a writer whose identity, Origen said, was known only to God.[1] Origen mentions, however, other traditions which had reached Alexandria, one assigning the writing of Hebrews to Clement, 'the bishop of the Romans', and

[1] See above, pp. 3 f., 10 f.

one assigning it to Luke, the evangelist and historian.[1] But Hebrews is not a translation, whatever it is; the assumption of an Aramaic or Hebrew original has no support in the language or style. And if the Epistle is not a translation of St. Paul's words, just as little can it be thought, with Origen, to be a commentary on his ideas, for the theology, as we have seen, has not the Pauline stamp. Nor can Hebrews be regarded as an original composition of any of the personalities who figure in these Alexandrian discussions. It cannot, for example, be assigned to Luke, because Luke belonged to Gentile, not to Jewish Christianity. It cannot be assigned to Clement, because Clement, though using the language of Hebrews at points as if it were his own, has ordinarily too pedestrian a style to have been capable of creating that masterpiece.

The only other great name put forward in antiquity as covering with its authority the Epistle to the Hebrews was that of Barnabas, to whom, as we have seen, the work was accredited by Tertullian, probably, as Zahn thinks, on the strength of a tradition received, like Tertullian's Montanism, from Asia Minor.[2] To this tradition no real exception can be taken on intrinsic grounds. Barnabas was a Jew. He can be presumed to have been a very cultured Jew. He belonged to the world-mission, and had been a member of the Pauline circle. He was a Levite from Cyprus, and he was known in the Church as a 'son of exhortation'.[3] On all counts he was what Tertullian calls him, *satis auctoratus vir*. But though the ascription of the Epistle to Barnabas is extraordinarily attractive on many

---

[1] Eusebius, *History*, VI. 25.
[2] Zahn, *Introduction to the New Testament*, II. pp. 302 ff.
[3] Acts iv. 36, xi. 22-25. Cf. Hebrews xiii. 22, ' Bear with this word of exhortation'.

grounds of internal probability, it is a striking illustration of the tantalising difficulty of the whole problem
that, even if the external attestation for Barnabas were
stronger than it is, this ascription does not meet all the
seeming requirements of the case.   It does not, for
example, support the on other grounds natural assumption that the writer was a Jew of Alexandria, versed in
the Jewish-Alexandrian theology, who had received
his institution in Christianity from followers of Stephen.
Barnabas was a Cypriote, and he had achieved eminence in the Church at Jerusalem before Stephen.   We
might get over these difficulties by the easy supposition
that, as an educated Jew of the Diaspora, Barnabas
had imbibed the quality and substance of the Alexandrian theology without being an Alexandrian, and
had, if not from the time of Stephen, at least from the
time of his memorable visit to Antioch, completely gone
over to the principles of Stephen and the world-mission.
Even so, there would remain the difficulty that no
evidence exists for connecting Barnabas with Rome
and with the Church there.   Certainly Clement in the
next generation (c. A.D. 95) cannot have known Barnabas, any more than Paul or Apollos, to be the author
of a document so familiar to him as Hebrews, or he
would surely not have been silent regarding him in
writing to the Corinthian Church.

The silence of Clement on this subject, despite the
fact that he knew and used the Epistle, is only to be
explained if we assume that either the authorship was
quite unknown to him, or was linked with some name
not familiar to the contemporary Church.   This
excludes the ascription of the work to Apollos, an
ascription supported in later times by Martin Luther,
but not attested in antiquity.   Apollos would admirably

suit the part in point of his Jewish-Alexandrian origin and training, but if Apollos had been the author, it is difficult to think that the Alexandrian Church would not have preserved some knowledge of the fact in view of the distinguished role of this son of Alexandria in the world-mission, and that Clement would not have mentioned him in writing to the Corinthians in whose history Apollos had played a notable part. Nor do we know of any connection of Apollos with Rome. Other modern attempts to discover the writer's identity have no greater interest than a parlour-game. It may be some compensation for our ignorance, however, to have it brought home to us that Early Christianity was even richer in creative minds and personalities than the exiguous surviving evidence of tradition gives us to understand.

CHARACTER OF THE CHURCH AT ROME. ST. PAUL'S EPISTLE TO THE ROMANS

At various points in our discussion of the Epistle to the Hebrews, the opinion has been expressed that the early Christian community at Rome, to a section of which Hebrews was written, was predominantly Jewish-Christian in composition and character. This judgment, to which the present writer has come principally on the ground of St. Paul's Epistle to the Romans, runs contrary to the conclusion ordinarily favoured by modern commentators on Romans. The latter believe that St. Paul had in mind a predominantly Gentile Church. The counter-position which is here affirmed does not deny that the Church at Rome contained a Gentile-Christian admixture, possibly a very large

Gentile-Christian admixture, but maintains that St. Paul's manner of approach to it suggests on every page that he thought of that Church primarily in terms of its Jewish heredity and ethos. The principal ground on which I base this opinion has been repeatedly urged in the foregoing chapters. It is the absence from both Hebrews and Romans of all reference to gnosticising or pagan Hellenistic errors such as are charged by St. Paul upon other Churches. It is now necessary to establish this position more broadly by subjecting the Epistle to closer critical inspection.

When St. Paul states at the opening of the great Epistle (i. 5-6) that he has received the grace of apostleship in order 'to promote obedience to the faith among all the Gentiles (*ethne*)', it is not necessarily implied that the persons addressed were themselves *ethne*, nor does that conclusion need to be drawn from the immediately following words, 'among whom you also are'. All that needs to be inferred is that the persons in question were geographically located in the region of the world to which the Jews gave the overhead name of the *ethne*. St. Paul was conscious of a commission to preach to the ethnic world. It is this that gives him his title to address himself to all Christians in that area, irrespective of whether they are Jews or Gentiles. When, a few lines later, he writes (i. 14-15), 'I am under obligation both to Greeks and barbarians . . . hence the readiness on my part to preach the gospel to you too at Rome', it might appear that the 'you too' involves the inclusion of the Roman Christians under one or other of these ethnic categories, but this is by no means certain. St. Paul in his delicate approach to this Church, which was not founded by himself, is obviously casting about for grounds to justify his action in addressing himself to it, and the words 'you too' may, as a matter of fact, reveal a sense that the persons addressed do not strictly belong in the narrower sense to either of these ethnic divisions of humanity, but are only domiciled among them. It is to be noticed that in the next verse (i. 16) the Apostle thinks it not irrelevant to say that his gospel 'is for the Jew first and also for the Greek'. The door is at least left open, therefore, for the possibility that the community in question presented to the Apostle a Jewish-Christian façade.

In the second half of chapter i. (verses 18-22), where St. Paul surveys the religious and moral condition of the contemporary Gentile world, it is to be observed that all the references to the *ethne* are in the *third* person: the *ethne* are the 'They'. But when at the beginning of the next chapter the Apostle turns by a gradual transition from the Gentiles to the Jews, the *second* personal pronoun enters: the Jew is 'Thou', and so throughout the chapter (ii. 1-16). In the succeeding passage (ii. 17-29) the Jew is definitely named as the possessor of the glorious privileges there summarised (ii. 17-20), and the Apostle brings home to him the solemn responsibilities of his favoured position. This emphasis on the Jew as 'Thou' admits at least of the special explanation that the Apostle is thinking either of the Jew who is in every Christian among the persons addressed, or of the unconverted Jews who form the background or fringe of the Church. In the next section (iii. 1-20), where St. Paul takes up the question of 'the advantage of the Jew', it is difficult to think of the question as having relevance to any body of hearers except a Jewish-Christian one. Gentile Christians would not be particularly interested in the question, and St. Paul can hardly be thought to be discussing the matter merely because of its theoretical interest or its importance to himself.

Next we have the passage (iii. 21-26) on the 'Righteousness of God' as something revealed 'apart from the Law', though witnessed to 'by the Law and the prophets'. St. Paul's interpretation of the Atonement here is more closely related—witness the term *hilasterion*—to the central ritual idea of the Jewish sacrificial cultus than anywhere else in his Epistles, and this fact has surely some suggestiveness. Also the discussion which is appended and which brings in the question, 'Or is God the God of the Jews only?' (iii. 29), and the concern of the Apostle to show that through faith we 'establish the Law' (iii. 31), while they aim at proving the universality of the gospel, would seem to indicate that the Jew is all the time uppermost in the Apostle's mind as he writes to this particular community at Rome.

At the beginning of the next chapter (iv. 1) we have the remarkable expression 'Abraham, our progenitor after the flesh'. Gentile Christians are children of Abraham according to the Spirit, but the persons here addressed have that status apparently by natural descent. It will not do to say that the Apostle is here claiming that descent only for himself or only for such other Jewish-born Christians as may happen to be at Rome. The words 'Abraham, our progenitor according to natural descent' must have some solid and substantial relevance to the extraction of the community as a whole. It is true that presently in the same chapter (iv. 9-15) the blessing bestowed on Abraham is deliberately given an interpretation which turns it in the direction of Gentile believers, but this bearing of the promise declares something which all Christians need to learn and remember—for Jewish and Gentile Christians stand on the same footing before the justifying grace of God. It does not prove that the Christians addressed are themselves Gentile Christians. But there were Gentile Christians among them, and Jewish Christians needed to be reminded of the universal range of grace even more than Gentile. The concluding words of the chapter which remind the readers that saving faith like Abraham's is faith in the God of the Resurrection (iv. 23-25) have as much importance for Jewish as for Gentile believers.

Nothing in chapter v. calls for special attention as bearing on our problem until we come to the verse near the close (v. 26) where St. Paul writes: 'And the Law came in by the way, that the lapse (or fall of man) might attain to its full dimensions.' While St. Paul would everywhere insist on this truth about the Law—for it belonged to the very essence of his understanding of the divine economy of revelation—the statement would be specially pertinent in a dialectical approach to Jewish Christians who, as he says elsewhere in the lettter (vii. 1), 'know what Law is'.

In chapter vi. we come for the first time in Romans upon an exposition of what is ordinarily called the 'Christ-mysticism' of the Apostle, his doctrine of the faith-union of the believer with Christ (vi. 1-14). But it is to be noted that the argument turns wholly upon the nature and meaning of baptism, and baptism was a rite which the Jew as well as the Gentile received as the sacrament of his incorporation into the Church. Even in Judaism baptism had been developed in a mystical direction, if, that is, inferences are to be drawn from the Jewish practice of proselyte-baptism as the admission-rite or initiation of converts into a share in the redemption effected for Israel at the Exodus.[1] It is to be observed that St. Paul confines his mysticism at this point strictly within the meaning of the sacrament in question, and in view of the existence of the Jewish analogy of proselyte baptism there is no justification for the view that the Apostle must have been here writing to Gentile Christians to whom mystical notions were familiar. Nor, later on in the chapter (vi. 15-23), can it be argued that the sins against which the Apostle inveighs as contrary to 'sanctification', specifically indicate a Gentile-Christian community. While the sins of impurity and lawlessness appear in the list of ethnic vices (i. 24 f.), they also figure among the things for which Jews are reproached (ii. 21-24), so that nothing, one way or another, is proved by these allusions.

In chapter vii. the opening words, 'I speak to those who know what Law is', suggest surely persons with an experience rooted in Judaism. While Gentiles have an inward law given to them (ii. 14-15) by which they are exercised, it is doubtful if the workings of this principle on the Gentile conscience could produce a spiritual history of the kind which St. Paul delineates in this chapter as life under the Law. Even if that doubt should be resisted, the candour and the intimacy of the Apostle's revelation of the character of that life are better explained if we suppose him to be writing to Christians who shared in some real degree his own inheritance and spiritual history. St. Paul is not here, or anywhere else, talking into the air. It is because we so often think of him as talking theology in the

---

[1] Cf. 1 Corinthians x. 1-2, and see W. L. Knox, *St. Paul and the Church of the Gentiles* (1939), pp. 28 f., 97 f., etc., and W. D. Davies, *Paul and Rabbinic Judaism* (1948), pp. 121 f.

M

abstract, and not as *ad homines* and *ad rem*, that we fail to evaluate the historical bearing of much of his teaching. When he speaks of experience under the Law, we are willing enough to recognise the Jew who is still in Paul himself, but we forget to ask whether Paul would have chosen to speak in this strain to *others* unless he was thinking of the Jew who was also in each one of them.

It is true that in the Galatian Epistle he speaks intimately of the same experience in addressing Christians of Gentile extraction, but in the Galatian Churches Judaising teachers had intruded themselves, and St. Paul had to expose the fallacy of their legal pretensions. In Romans there is no reference to such intrusion from outside, and we are left to the conclusion that the Apostle, in analysing the nature of moral life under the Law, is taking his stand on knowledge which he assumes his readers to possess in virtue of their pre-Christian experience.

In chapter viii. we pass from the pre-Christian or sub-Christian stage of life to the new stage of life in the Spirit, and St. Paul uses a language applicable to all Christians, so that nothing in this chapter bears on the distinction of Jewish and Gentile elements in the Church. All distinctions are swallowed up in the unity of the confession 'Abba, Father', to which we are brought by the Spirit of God (viii. 14-17). Yet even here St. Paul can speak of the 'law' of the Spirit of life in Christ Jesus (viii. 2). The passage is extraordinarily significant:

> 'The law of the Spirit of life in Christ Jesus has made me (*v.l.* thee) free from the law of sin and death.'

Is this merely *the Jew in Paul* trying to interpret Chris-

tianity to others, and applying the word law to the
vital principle of the Christian life because it is instinctive in *him* to express the nature of all religion in
terms of law? Or is it Paul attempting to interpret
Christianity to *the Jew in others*, and therefore employ-
ing a language which *they* can understand? Probably
it is both. The Apostle in any case believes that the
language which, as an ex-Jew, he uses to explain his
own experience will also be intelligible to those to whom
he writes.

In chapters ix.-xi. we have what perhaps is the
innermost core of the Epistle to the Romans, St. Paul's
exposition of what may be called the Righteousness of
God in history. The section is concerned to explicate
the tragedy of the 'casting away' of God's people
Israel, and nowhere in the Apostle's writings have we
so passionate a revelation of his yearning for the
salvation of the Jews (ix. 1-3, x. 1), of his sense of the
glory of Israel's religious calling and endowment (ix.
4-5), and of his own feeling of solidarity with his race
and nation (ix. 3, xi. 1). It is not necessary to enter
here into the substance and the details of his great
argument. No one doubts the intense reality of St.
Paul's sense of solidarity with Israel. The question
which concerns us at this point is why St. Paul chooses
to deal with this particular question in the Epistle to
the Romans. It is not a problem which he has tackled
in any other of his letters. If it be answered that he
treats the problem here because it is germane to the
main general theme of the Epistle, which is the Righteousness of God, we may push the question a stage
further back and ask why he makes the Righteousness
of God the special theme of the Epistle to the Romans.
Can we think of him doing this merely to give the

Romans a fully rounded, systematic summary of his teaching as a whole? And does he introduce this section on Israel purely to relieve his own mind on a sorely felt, and sorely baffling personal problem? However great such urges may have been, it is at least a tenable proposition that the Apostle is led to deal with these matters on this occasion through his sense of a particular opportunity or challenge confronting him at his approach to the Roman Church. Such an opportunity or challenge would certainly be present if he had reason to regard that Church as predominantly Jewish-Christian in its heredity or outlook or mentality. On the other hand, neither the choice of the general theme of the Epistle, nor the engagement of his mind with the particular problem of the casting away of Israel would equally explain themselves if the Roman Church mainly consisted of elements drawn from Gentile society. Gentile Christians would not feel the same concern over what had happened to the Jewish people. When St. Paul writes to definitely ethnic Churches, he starts from other themes, e.g. from the Wisdom of God in 1 Corinthians, or from the freedom of the gospel in Galatians, and he does not handle in such Epistles the very grievous question of Israel's fate.

On the other hand, that question and the problem of its relation to the Righteousness of God in history would press very greatly indeed on the minds of Jewish Christians in so powerful a centre of Jewish influence as Rome.

The Church at Rome, however, is not wholly Jewish-Christian. There is a Gentile-Christian section, and possibly a very considerable one. St. Paul, who is not only an 'Israelite' (xi. 1) but an 'apostle of the Gentiles'

who magnifies his office (xi. 13), rejoices that the—for
him temporary and provisional—rejection of unbelieving Judaism has, in the divine plan, made room for
'the reconciliation of the world' through the bringing
of the *ethne* into the people of God. He stresses this
inclusiveness of the gospel (x. 12-15). Towards the
close of the great argument (xi. 13-24) he turns directly
to the Gentile section in the Church, and reminding
them of their privileged position as 'grafted' into the
olive tree of Israel (xi. 17-18), he asks them not to vaunt
over the broken-off branches. The words in which he
does so are remarkable:

> 'It is not you who carry the root, but the root carries
> you.'

Ordinarily we suppose St. Paul to mean that it is not
the Gentile Christianity of the world that represents
the original stock of the Church, but Jewish Christianity. But is it not more pertinent and relevant in
the context to interpret the words rather in this way:
it is not you Roman-Gentile Christians who constitute
the stock of the Church at Rome, but your Jewish-
Christian brethren? This makes excellent sense, and
its admission as St. Paul's meaning here puts the
finishing touch to the argument which we have been
constructing.

In chapter xii. we are again at a level where the
distinctions of Jew and Gentile disappear, but in the
succeeding chapter it may very reasonably be contended that the injunctions to respect the authority
of the civil government (xiii. 1-5) and to pay taxes
(xiii. 6-7) point to Jewish-born anti-imperial tendencies
on the part of those addressed. The references to the
sins of drinking and sensuality to which we come later

in the chapter (xiii. 13) are no absolute evidence to the contrary. These undoubtedly represent weaknesses to which Gentiles were prone, but there were Gentiles in the community in any case, and therefore these allusions need not upset our general thesis with regard to the main stock of the Roman Church.

There remains the evidence of chapters xiv. and xv. which present some hitherto unmentioned features in the Roman situation. A *minority* here appears within the Church, characterised by scruples or particularist views on the subjects of foods and holy days; it considers certain foods as forbidden and certain days as specially holy (xiv. 1-6). It is not necessary to go into the whole nature of the problem which is here presented, nor into St. Paul's mode of dealing with it. The Apostle is definitely critical of the principles of the minority (xiv. 17-18), but he urges charity and brotherliness on the part of the 'strong', who undoubtedly represent the core of the Church and the true line of the development of 'faith'. But he strongly deprecates party-feeling and division and exhorts to unity for the glory and honour of God (xv. 5-7), emphasising the universal embrace of a salvation which brings the Gentiles into the Church along with the Jews (xv. 8-13).

The primary question we have here to consider is, Was this scrupulous minority, which in any case appears to be Jewish-Christian by its emphasis on food-laws and holy days, the whole Jewish-Christian constituency in a larger mixed Church, or was it a sub-division of that Jewish-Christian constituency? In view of the fact that, as we have seen, the general evidence of the Epistle suggests that St. Paul was consciously writing to a Church that was Jewish-Christian in the main, we seem justified in preferring the latter alternative. The scrupulous minority was *a sub-section of the Jewish-Christian core* of the Church. In favour of this view may also be adduced the evidence of the very striking passage:

> 'I say that Christ became a minister to the circum-
> cised for the sake of God's truth, i.e. to confirm
> the promises to the fathers, and that the Gentiles
> might glorify God for His mercy' (xv. 8-9).

The argument is interesting: Just as Christ came to the Jews, that through His ministry the Jews might have the ancient promises fulfilled to them, and the Gentiles at the same time have reason to glorify God for the share now accorded to them in so great a blessing, so St. Paul exhorts the Jewish Christians at Rome so to exemplify the charity of Christ in their relations with the dissident minority as to hold and keep them in the unity of the Church, and at the same time give the Gentile Christians among them cause once again to give glory to God for their own inclusion in the Church. If I am right in offering this inter-pretation, the various elements in the Church at Rome fall at last into proper perspective and proportion.

1. The Roman-Christian community is Jewish (i.e. Jewish-Hellenist) in the main.

2. This Jewish-Hellenist community includes a 'Hebrew' minority (regarding which we have fuller light in the Epistle to the Hebrews).

3. There is also an observing Gentile-Christian section.

And St. Paul (xv. 14-21) takes this predominantly Jewish-Christian Church into his confidence in the hope of bespeaking its understanding sympathy and co-operation in the world-wide task which he executes as 'priest' (*leitourgos*) of Christ Jesus to the Gentiles.

THE EPISTLE TO THE HEBREWS AND THE OLD TESTAMENT

Our examination of the hortatory and didactic sections of the Epistle in Chapters III-V will have shown the close and continuous dependence of the writer's mind on the sacred records of the Jewish religion, and in this particular his exposition of Christianity stands in more positive relation to that religion than the teaching of either St. Paul or the Johannine evangelist. In the figures, types, institutions and personalities of the old economy of grace he sees the manifestation of God in Christ foreshadowed at every point; the Old Testament religion was provisional, prophetic, symbolic, premonitory, pointing beyond itself. The form of the later revelation was present, if not yet the substance. Yet at one important point the metaphor of the shadow employed by the writer is in need of explication. Shadow may suggest something which in itself is unreal or even deceptive as in the Platonic philosophy. But the writer to the Hebrews is not primarily a Platonic idealist but an eschatologist, and when he says (x. 1) that the Law had in it the shadow of the Christian order, though not the reality, he means that the new order was at hand, at the door, projecting itself on the plane of the Old Testament history, announcing its advent. The history, the Law, and the cultus of Israel were to this extent witnesses in advance to the Christian salvation.

Thus when Moses forsook the court of Egypt to cast in his lot with his Hebrew brethren, the writer declares that he thereby chose the reproach of 'the Christ' (xi. 25-26), and this, as we have seen, not in a merely analogical but in a real sense.[1] The Christ, the pre-incarnate Son of God, was actually, though invisibly, an agent and participant in the redemption effected for Israel at the Exodus, and Moses by his decision of faith was sharing in the Saviour's passion. He was already identified with the Christian people of God. So also when, dealing with the writer's conception of the cloud of 'witnesses' (xii. 1), we repelled the suggestion that the types of faith depicted in chapter xi. were sub-Christian, we did so on the sufficient grounds (a) that for the writer to the Hebrews the eschatological calling of God in the Old Testament was the same in form and principle as in the New, and (b) that for the same writer the Christ of God was veritably present and active in the history of Israel, so that the response of the heroes of faith to the promises given to Israel was in a real sense a response to Christ, towards whom their eyes were really directed when, as the writer says, they endured 'as seeing Him who is invisible'.[2]

The writer's thought of the pre-incarnate Saviour as present in the revelation of God granted under the old order is reinforced and illustrated by his interpretation of Psalms and other texts from the Old Testament records. His use of Psalm xcvii. 7 (LXX) is a case in point. The singer's words: 'Let all the angels of God worship Him' are given a direct meaning with reference to the Firstborn of God, and the introductory formula: 'When He brings the Firstborn into the world, etc.', conveys the interpretation that God's summons to the angels to worship the Son revealed the Incarnation as already present in the mind of God and as already

---

[1] See above, pp. 79 f.   [2] Above, pp. 81 f., 96, 144.

announced to the world.[1] Similarly the use made of
the trio of Old Testament passages, Psalm xxii. 22,
Isaiah viii. 17, 18, the words of which are made to
refer to the brethren of Christ, shows that where
psalmists and prophets spoke, the overtones were those
of the pre-existent Son of God.[2] In the same way,
when the 'man' or 'son of man' of the Eighth Psalm
is recognised as Jesus, there is involved the assumption
that it was of Jesus that the psalmist actually spoke.[3]
On the same principle of interpretation again it is the
voice of the Messiah-Son of God that is to be heard in
such passages as Proverbs viii. 22-31, Ecclesiasticus
xxiv., and Wisdom vii. 21, etc., in which the activities
of the Divine Wisdom in creation and providence are
declared and attested to the world.[4]

The most remarkable instance, however, of the
writer's Christological interpretation of the Old Testament is his use of the passage, Psalm xl. 6-8, where the
LXX reading 'A body hast Thou prepared for me',
taken with the response, 'Lo, I come to do Thy will',
is construed as an announcement of the Saviour's
acceptance of His Incarnation, which acceptance,
therefore, dates from His pre-existent life, and is
affirmed, so to speak, overhead of the psalmist.[5] This
right to recognise the overtones of Christ in the Old
Testament revelation has a place in the faith of the
writer to the Hebrews which, had he known the tests
applied to that literature by the historical and exegetical
science of a later day, would not have seemed to him
to be invalidated in any real sense. He would have
allowed that such Biblical criticism had a function to
fulfil on the plane of what he called the 'shadow', but

---

[1] See above, pp. 92 f.   [2] Above, p. 102.   [3] Above, pp. 98 f.
[4] Above, pp. 96 f.   [5] Above, pp. 144 f.

he would not have considered it to exclude the right of Christian faith to receive and affirm those deeper involutions of truth which come to light in the Old Testament when looked at in respect of its 'substance'.

It is in accordance with this finding of Christ in the Old Testament by an act of faith which is not conditioned by the conclusions of strict historical interpretation that we may now discover the full range of the truth covered by the writer's statement (xiii. 8):

'Jesus Christ is the same, yesterday, today, and for ever.'

In the context, where the writer is speaking of the memorable record and noble end of the earlier leaders of the Roman-Christian community, the word 'yesterday' admits certainly of direct application to the first age of the Church, to which these leaders belonged and of which they were the products. But his pre-occupation with the larger aspects of the Christology of Scripture gives the declaration that 'Jesus Christ is the same' a vaster range of meaning. Look back on the entire history of the people of God, he seems to say to us, and you will find no past, no yesterday, in which the Christ of God has not been present and active; look forward to the future, and again there will be no period when He will not be there—an entirely Christological and eschatological interpretation of history! In Jesus Christ eternity is manifested in time.

THE EPISTLE TO THE HEBREWS AND THE EVANGELICAL TRADITION

It is, however, the 'today' of the Christian revelation as centred in the Incarnation which forms the core and

all-essential substance of the writer's presentation.
Apart from the Epistle to the Hebrews we should not
have known the greatness of the place which the
Incarnation of the Son of God held in the gospel of the
world-mission of the first age of the Church. At the
time when the Epistle was written the Synoptic Gospels
were not in being. The material, indeed, out of which
they later took shape was present in solution in the
minds of the teachers and leaders of the Church, and
was used in their preaching. The tradition was borne
everywhere at the heart of the world-mission, and it
was in the course of that mission and as essential instru-
ments of its propaganda that the Gospels were written,
Mark probably at Rome, Matthew almost certainly at
Antioch, Luke at some other centre, possibly in Mace-
donia or Achaea. And the Pauline, Petrine, and
Johannine books of the New Testament, as well as
Hebrews, attest the wide diffusion and influence of the
same tradition. But whereas St. Paul can draw a
distinction between a first stadium of revelation in
which the Son of God was manifested 'after the flesh',
and a second stadium dating from the Resurrection,
in which He is revealed 'after the Spirit' (Romans i.
3-4), and can even say *à propos* of the two stages that
'if we knew Christ after the flesh' (i.e. in His earthly
historical manifestation) 'we no longer know Him in
that manner' (2 Corinthians v. 16), the writer to the
Hebrews knows no such distinction. For him *the
Eternal Spirit is not something which in its operation
casts all that happened before the death and resurrection
of Jesus into the shadow, and so transcends it, but is
rather the revelatory power and principle which holds
the Incarnate Life for ever before us in its inexhaustible
wealth of transcendent meaning, so that we see Jesus*

crowned with glory for the suffering of death (ii. 9).
In justice to St. Paul we should not press too strongly
the distinction to which we have referred, for it may be
thought to rest ultimately on the development of his
subjective apprehension of Christ in the pre-conversion
and post-conversion periods of his experience rather
than on any objective differences between the pre-
Resurrection and post-Resurrection modes of the
Saviour's manifestation. But the fact that St. Paul at
times can set flesh and spirit in antithesis with reference
to the modes of the Christ-manifestation indicates that
a certain subjective limitation cleaves to Paulinism,
which has had some ill results in Christian history.
From this limitation the writer to the Hebrews is
happily free.—But has he done the same justice as
St. Paul to the glory and power of the Resurrection of
Christ and to its transforming results in Christian life?
That is another question.

For the moment we must leave aside this last question. Our immediate concern is with the fact that
in Hebrews the very heart of the Christian revelation
is in the spectacle of the Incarnate Life by which the
Son of God was qualified in the school of suffering to
be our High-Priest, and to make His supreme Oblation.
Nor could the reality of the experience and the intensity
of the conflict be more vividly presented than in the
passage, chapter v. 7-8. Here is no Docetic manifestation, nor union of God with man which excludes
a human will, human passions, human temptations, a
full human personality. In this and in other ways the
teaching of Hebrews comes at concrete points into
close parallelism with the matter of the Synoptic tradition with which we are concerned at the moment.

First, there is in Hebrews a consistently eschatological presentation of the norm of the Christian life and calling. The mind of the writer is oriented to an ultimate goal towards which the Christian is to strive with unrelaxed and increasing tension, the life of the Age to Come. So the Jesus of the Synoptic tradition called men to follow Him in preparation for the Kingdom of God which He announced to be at the door. He brought His followers face to face, in every moment of life's decisions, with the absolute nature of the will of God to reign. He thereby compelled a tension in their souls which only the coming of the supreme and final event of the Kingdom could resolve. They were placed in a situation—the Sermon on the Mount in St. Matthew's Gospel illustrates its nature—in which to go backwards was to renounce the salvation of God, to go forwards was eternal life. Though the writer to the Hebrews does not speak of the Christian crisis in terms of the Lord's *teaching*, his presentation of the Christian calling turns on precisely identical issues. To be 'partakers with Christ' requires that men maintain their initial decision of faith firmly and to the end, no matter what consequences are involved (iii. 14).

Secondly, the writer to the Hebrews knows no *final* formula under which to bring the Christian life except that of martyrdom for Christ's sake or of preparedness for that eventuality. Christians are summoned to go forth to Jesus 'without the camp', bearing His reproach (xiii. 13). The words 'You have not yet resisted to blood in your conflict against sin' (xiii. 4) suggests that for him the last sacrifice comes definitely into the prospect which lies before the faithful. So the Jesus of the Synoptic Gospels at the Messianic crisis in His ministry demanded of His Galilean followers, whom

He had called to seek the Kingdom of God, that they should hazard even life itself in fidelity to Him (Mark viii. 34). The words were spoken primarily to the Twelve, who only on the terms of leaving every earthly interest and security behind could accompany Jesus on the last journey to Jerusalem, but Mark says that Jesus addressed the call to the multitude as well, and Luke says that He spoke to all (Luke ix. 23). Hebrews in its interpretation of the eschatological calling stands in the closest agreement at this point with the norm of Christian life outlined in the Synoptic teaching.

Thirdly, the supreme illustration of the close congruence of Hebrews with the Synoptic tradition is, of course, the centrality of place given to the human experience of Jesus in 'the days of His flesh'. On this subject nothing need be added here except that, whereas the Synoptic evangelists present the features of that drama objectively, without other comment on its nature than is given in the word of Jesus about the 'necessity' of the Son of Man's suffering, the writer to the Hebrews reflects on the intrinsic character of the experience, the tremendous psychological reality of the self-identification of the Christ with sinners, the supreme moral *fitness* of the revelation of the divine-human relation so given. 'It befitted God', so he writes, 'in bringing many sons to glory, to make the Hero of their salvation perfect through sufferings' (ii. 10). 'Obligation lay on Jesus', he continues, 'to be assimilated to His brethren in all things that He might become a compassionate and faithful High-Priest in the service of God for the expiation of the sins of His people' (ii. 17). In this emphasis on the moral nature of the factors predetermining the character of the divine-human encounter in the Christian revelation we have the fullest approximation in the New Testament to a *rationale* of the Atonement, and it constitutes a divination unique even in that literature, one which takes shape, moreover, at the highest level of spiritual realisation, and which gives the Epistle to the Hebrews a singular power of appeal to an age which, like our own, has experienced the full brunt of the critical attack on all that is abstract and impersonal in the tenets of the received theology.

The Epistle to the Hebrews and St. Paul

At a whole series of points in our argument there has been occasion to institute comparisons between the teaching of Hebrews and that of St. Paul. We have been driven on constant cross-reference to the Apostle's letters by the very necessity of bringing to articulate expression the special character of the theology of Hebrews, and the results have been sufficient to demonstrate that the two modes of presenting the gospel indicate parallel channels in the course of the world-mission of Christianity as it poured itself out on the life of the world in the apostolic age. There is a remarkable symmetry or similarity in the patterns or general categories within which the gospel is presented by the two writers, but there is a difference with regard to the matter which is stamped with, or enclosed within these forms. The streams are parallel in their courses, but the *terrain* or bed over which they run is not identical. While it is not necessary to recapitulate the points of interesting concurrence which have been noted in the two presentations, something should be said with regard to a number of outstanding points of divergence.

1. While St. Paul presents the gospel primarily in terms of its antithesis to the law of Judaism as a code of righteousness, Hebrews is engaged with its relation to the cultus as apparatus of grace.[1] To some extent the difference of front may be explained by variations in the religious situation presented in diverse sectors of the world-mission Church, but in part it goes back to differences in the initial approach to the Christian realities of two dissimilar minds. The advantage of setting the two presentations side by side is that there is thus afforded us a more stereoscopic view of the teaching and fortunes of the world-mission than would have been possible if we were dependent on only one of the two. We are able, by means of the comparison, to supplement and check the one system of thought by the other, and this is of great consequence alike for the theologian and for the historian.

2. There is disparity again with regard to the relation in which the Christian order stands to the old order of religion as a whole. St. Paul, as we have seen,[2] in preaching Christ insists instinctively on the essential paradox of the Christian salvation, its incommensurability with all Jewish and, in general, with all human expectation. A crucified Messiah is to the Jews a scandal, an insuperable obstacle and affront to faith. For the writer to the Hebrews, on the other hand, the Passion of Christ is no bewildering paradox but comes as the climax and fulfilment of the truth that was adumbrated and the grace that was operative in the now superseded economy. There is no intellectual offence of the Cross in Hebrews but only the moral one,

---

[1] See above, pp. 19 f., etc.   [2] Above, pp. 114-116, etc.

N

that by the self-oblation of Jesus we are pointed inexorably 'beyond the camp' to a new heavenly life. So also for the same writer the distinction between the old and the new Israel, the old and the new covenants, is not of a kind to be expressed by the Pauline antithesis, absolute in its nature, of flesh and spirit, death and life.[1]   Perhaps St. Paul had encountered the actuality of the Jewish intolerance of the gospel more poignantly than our author who lived more in the serene air of Old Testament prophecy and typology. But each has seized an aspect of the truth, and it can be said that wisdom is justified at this point by both of her children.

It goes with the above distinction, however, that in the Epistle to the Hebrews there is less sense than in St. Paul of the essential newness, relatively to the older order, of the life begun in Christ.   Commenting at an earlier stage of the argument on the Pauline tendency to set flesh and spirit in antithesis with reference even to the modes of the Saviour's manifestation,[2] we noted the presence of a subjective element in St. Paul from which the writer to the Hebrews was free.   But we raised the question at the same moment whether the latter had done the same justice as St. Paul to the glory and transforming power of the Resurrection of Christ as an element in the Christian revelation of grace.   If, now, this question has to be answered in the negative, the reason for the comparative recession of the Resurrection in the writer's thought has also come to light. The Resurrection of the Saviour—see the great passage, xiii. 20-21—is recognised as a moment in the fulfilment of God's eschatological purpose for His redeemed, but does not mark an absolute crisis with respect to the

---

[1] See above, pp. 114-116, 129.   [2] Above, pp. 153-154.

nature of our calling. The writer does not think of Christians as risen with Christ, but as followers of a risen and heavenly Redeemer, who will participate with Him at the last, and this connects with a general determination of the whole of the writer's religious thinking to which we must now recur.

3. Within the sphere of the Christian religion there is a marked contrast between the mind of St. Paul, instinctively stressing at every point of his Atonement-doctrine the love of God, the love of Christ, the union of the soul with Christ, the destruction of the sinful flesh, the power of the Spirit, the peace of believing, and, on the other hand, the mind of the writer to the Hebrews, conscious of the dread aspects of the Christian manifestation of God, for whom God is a consuming fire. For St. Paul it is imperative to grasp and present the redeemed relation of the soul to God in terms of present achieved status, inward possession and rest, the deliverance of the soul from the burden of condemnation, the triumphant victory of prevailing grace. For the writer to the Hebrews the Christian life is a tense and unending conflict which finds resolution and rest only at the End. While the difference is not absolute, since at points the attitudes interpenetrate each other, yet in the main it holds, and it may be summarised by saying that while the writer to the Hebrews is essentially an eschatologist, St. Paul at the centre of his being is a mystic. To some extent, as we have seen, the two attitudes can be taken to an explanation in differences in the historical approach of the two men to the Christian realities. To some extent, however, the duality is rooted in the complex nature of all religious reality in respect of the object of belief as it confronts the soul.

N*

Whatever judgment may be passed on particular features in Dr. Rudolf Otto's analysis of the primordial nature of the numinous experience, an indisputable truth underlies his differentiation of the two aspects of the experience, which he designates respectively as the *tremendum* and the *fascinans*, taken with the corresponding reactions of the worshipping spirit. On the one hand he notices our dread sense of confrontation by something which repels us, holds us off, challenges our security and our very existence, but by which also at the higher levels of religious experience our affections are 'raised and solemnised'. On the other hand is an attraction which draws the soul to impel itself towards the numinous object, to appropriate it, to merge its existence in it, to identify it with itself. The first attitude attains its highest sublimation and purest expression in the religion of the Bible as a whole, the second is illustrated in the character of Hellenistic pagan mysticism. Without further elaboration of the details of Otto's analysis, we may recognise the distinction of the two reactions in the attitudes to the Christ-manifestation of the two minds we have been comparing. For St. Paul it is an absolute necessity, as we have noted, to think of the mighty acts of God in Christ, the Incarnation, Death, Resurrection, and Ascension to glory of the Son of God, as events to be immediately appropriated, realised, and re-enacted in the soul of the Christian: it is through this appropriation that the Christian comes to be 'in Christ'. Such mysticism is not natural to the mind of the writer to the Hebrews, being replaced in him by the conception of the soul's eternal objective confrontation by Christ. Christian existence is existence 'with Christ', a total direction of the soul's energies 'towards Christ'. Both determinations have their place, however, within the orbit of the Christian life.

EPILOGUE

If the interpretation which has been put upon Hebrews in the foregoing chapters is correct, the effect cannot but be to enrich and expand our conception both of early Christian evangelism and of early Christian history. We should not have known, apart from Hebrews, over how wide and varied a front the battle of Christianity was fought and won in the first age of the Church's life. It has sometimes been pled in favour of the modern interpretation of Hebrews which detaches the Epistle from its traditional Jewish-Christian setting and holds it to have been addressed to Gentile-Christians that the Christian theology of the period is thereby delivered from entanglement with issues which, since St. Paul, are taken to have been dead. But if the short-circuiting of historical theory which comes to light in the latter assumption has to go, it may be felt, as a real gain accruing from the counter-position which we have taken, that we see the Christian Church and theology more squarely and broadly built on the foundations of the Old Testament, and rising phoenix-like from the embers not only of Jewish legalism but of the Jewish means of grace.

INDEX

I

BIBLICAL PASSAGES

1. OLD TESTAMENT AND JEWISH LITERATURE

2. New Testament

II

GENERAL SUBJECTS